STRANGE BUT TRUE
# New York City

# STRANGE BUT TRUE
# New York City

## TALES OF THE BIG APPLE

S. B. Howard

## INSIDERS' GUIDE®

GUILFORD, CONNECTICUT
AN IMPRINT OF THE GLOBE PEQUOT PRESS

Produced in 2005 by
PRC Publishing
The Chrysalis Building
Bramley Road, London W10 6SP, UK

An imprint of Chrysalis Books Group plc

INSIDERS' GUIDE®    is a trademark of The Globe Pequot Press.

Cover and text design: Sean Walsh
Photo credits: front cover © Chrysalis Image Library/Simon Clay

        Library of Congress Cataloging-in-Publication

Howard, S. B.
  New York City : tales of the Big Apple / S. B. Howard.-- 1st ed.
    p. cm. -- (Strange but true)
  ISBN 0-7627-3679-8
  1. New York (N.Y.)–History–Anecdotes. 2. New York (N.Y.)--Social life and
customs--Anecdotes. 3. New York (N.Y.)--Biography–Anecdotes. 4. Curiosities and
wonders--New York (State)--New York--Anecdotes. I. Title. II. Strange but true
(Guilford, Conn.)

F128.36.H69 2005                                                    2004060917
974.7'1--dc22

Printed in Malaysia
First Edition/First Printing

# STRANGE BUT TRUE
# New York City

# Introduction

In 1524, the pirate and explorer John the Florentine, whose real name was Giovanni da Verrazano, was employed by King Francis I of France. When his ship was blown off course by a storm, he discovered New York Harbor. The world was never the same.

The contradiction of pirate and explorer may help explain the glorious, strange, peculiar, frustrating, remarkable, unique character that is New York to this day. It is a city of commerce and culture; of elegance and filth; of sophistication and provincialism; of uncountable wealth and unimaginable poverty. New York and the boroughs that comprise it—Manhattan, Staten Island, Bronx, Brooklyn, Queens—is an amalgam of cultures, tongues, perspectives, and ideologies, with people whose energy, creativity, and weirdness make life a daily adventure—or, more often, a misadventure.

A brief history of New York illustrates that the melting pot personality of the city—the critical cause of all that is and will ever be strange about New York—was there at the beginning. Despite Verrazano's discovery (recognized hundreds of years later, in 1964, when a bridge in his name was finally built connecting Staten Island to Brooklyn), France had other wars to fight. The Algonquin Indians who lived on the land later to be known as Manhattan (they called it *Manna-*

*Hata*, meaning "Hill Island" or "Island of the Hills") remained there undisturbed until the English seaman Henry Hudson was employed by the Dutch West India Company to search for a northeast trading passage to China. In 1609, Hudson's ship, *Half Moon*, anchored on what is now known as Sandy Hook, introduced alcohol and firearms to the Indians, and gave the Dutch West India Company a new trading passage, as desired.

The state of New York was called New Netherland, the city New Amsterdam, but few Dutch settled there. Rather, the city's first immigrants were refugees who had settled in Holland and then came to the New World, creating what is now Battery Park City by filling in the edges at the Hudson and East Rivers. In 1626, depending on the history book, either Peter Minuit or a man by the name of Willem Verhulst, the director of New Netherland, bought the land from the Algonquins for 60 guilders or 24 American dollars (Verhulst was later banished from the city for the crime of embezzlement). Then, in 1638, the first Anglo-Saxons arrived, and by 1643, there were 18 different languages spoken.

In 1653, a 13-foot log wall stretched from the two rivers, erected when Cromwell in England had declared war on the Dutch Republic. The wall was torn down in 1699. The area where the wall had been would become known as Wall Street. In 1664, the Dutch lost the new colony to the English and New Amsterdam became New York City, named for James Stuart, the duke of York.

For a long time, the southern tip of land defined New York City. Where the public library stands now at Fifth Avenue and 42nd Street was a reservoir serving the city. As the immigrant population increased, the city's boundary was pushed further and further north. Although Germans and Irish were the largest group of immigrants, Chinese, Latin Americans, and East Indians were among the diverse peoples who made up the growing populace of the city in the late 19th century, before the huge immigration explosion in the 1920s. Today, 40 percent of the more than eight million people who live in the five boroughs of New York City are immigrants.

With a variety of languages and cultures, but with a similar desire to build a new life in this new land, the immigrants gave New York City much that is glorious about it to this day. The ingenuity and inventiveness needed not only to survive but to thrive and prosper motivated these newcomers to create street lighting and sidewalks, air pollution laws, the first gas pipeline, and the city's first botanical garden called Elgin Garden (where Radio City Music Hall and Rockefeller Center, between Fifth and Sixth Avenues and 49th and 50th Streets, now stand). Neighborhoods were formed as immigrants sought out their fellow countrymen, but even so, by 1820, with a population of 391,000, most New Yorkers lived south of what is now 23rd Street. In fact, streets such as the Bowery, Canal, Pine, and Pearl—today part of Soho and the Wall Street area— were home to most of the populace. The 700 acres between what is now called Fifth and Eighth Avenues and 59th to 106th Street were unfit for housing, being farmland or swamps. In 1876, that much of uninhabitable space and more, up to 110th Street—843 magnificent acres—opened to the public as Central Park.

Eventually, New York City became headquarters for the British during the Seven Years' War beginning in 1756. And in 1776, even after the Declaration of Independence was signed, New York City remained under British control. In 1789, it even became the nation's capital for one year, and was the state capital until 1797. In time, horses gave way to hansom cabs, which gave way to the elevated trains. Bus lines were started and the subway system developed. The necessity of building up rather than out created a startling new urban landscape. A magnificent statue to Liberty was unveiled. New York City, always changing, yet somehow, always the same.

Over the years, New York has been home to a true *Who's Who* of people of achievement—some of it dubious achievement, indeed. From Theodore Roosevelt to Mark Twain, Katharine Hepburn to Norman Mailer, and Muhammad Ali, Mickey Mantle, Joe Namath, and Joe DiMaggio. Great artists like Leonard Bernstein, Marianne Moore, Agnes DeMille, Eugene O'Neill, Herman Melville, O. Henry, and Alvin Ailey; as well as men of stature such as Colin Powell and Dr. Jonas Salk. And of course Aaron Burr, John Jacob Astor, Walt Whitman, and Thomas Jefferson all called New York home at some point in their lifetimes. As did the Son of Sam, John Gotti, "Boss" Tweed, Lucky Luciano, and Meyer Lansky, among other notorious names. Some were natives, some made New York their adopted home, but none of them were untouched by it—the city with its vibrancy and its weaknesses imbuing their achievements.

The history of New York is so rich that an entire museum has been dedicated to it in Manhattan. A brief overview of this history is necessary to understand the present and the future of the city, because it is the history in the making, happening daily in the lives of New Yorkers, that gives New York its unique—and never forget—strange character. And that is part of the problem for those living in Brooklyn, the Bronx, Queens, and Staten Island. In 1897, all the boroughs were legally consolidated, comprising the 359 square miles of New York City. And while these four boroughs are home to unusual or laudable or laughable or unbelievable incidents and individuals, you never hear anyone say, "Oh, those great cities, London, Paris, Rome, Brooklyn." When one says, "New York," one immediately thinks of Manhattan.

New York inspires extremes of emotion and behavior. You either love it or you hate it; there is no in-between. Why, even the state's own governor doesn't bother to hide his animosity about it. You don't make the mistake of hoping to change it and survive. You learn to live by its rules—or you get out. Maybe to the outskirts of the quieter boroughs, or, shame that it is, to another county, state, or country.

New York City has attitude. No other major city in the world, with the exception perhaps of Paris, has this much cool confidence and lets natives and tourists alike know it and feel it. Many New Yorkers are provincial, earnestly believing that life ceases west of the Hudson River, except for the occasional squeak to be noticed from Los Angeles. London has its theatre, Paris its fashion, Rome its pope, but New Yorkers truly believe their city is bigger or better or smarter or more sophisticated, or, in the case of the Catholic Church, more Catholic.

The lack of modesty New Yorkers feel for their home is both commendable and ridiculous, and helps foment the jealousy and hatred outsiders feel for the city. Yet the people of New York—the people of all the boroughs of New York—can pull together during times of crisis much like the volunteer firemen of a small farm community. Death of a beloved hero, tragedy from the skies, blackouts, blizzards, or strikes—New Yorkers cope better than anyone. And only in New York do they cope with humor.

Because that is what is so magnificent about New York—it is a place that makes you reach for the best in yourself or risk the consequences. New York is tough—if you don't help yourself, it won't help you. It has no time for slackers, which may be why everything is so fast, so energetic. It's not easy living in New York. There's dirt and crime and incredible expenses—and worst of all, there are too many people living in too small a space. Ride a bus or subway in New York, and you'll find English is the second language. Try to see the Christmas tree at Rockefeller Center in person and you may call yourself an idiot. Live here long enough and you, too, will curse the damn tourists who think they can stand on 34th and Fifth and look up, oblivious to the pedestrians around them. Know a bike messenger would as soon run you down with an expletive not-deleted as follow the traffic rules.

But if a stranger asks for directions, especially if he happens to be from another country, a New Yorker will try to help. A blind man and his seeing-eye dog at the street corner? You can bet a New Yorker will ask if he needs assistance. Lost pet sign posted on a lamppost? The whole neighborhood will be in on the search. New Yorkers are really no different than people anywhere else—there are just more of them who don't speak to each other.

It is inevitable, therefore, that over the years of increases in population and cultural diversity, New York has become even more New York-y— meaning more quirky and more unique. In a place of over 8 million inhabitants, there are no doubt 8 million incredible, unbelievable, but totally true events, tales, or trivia. And that is where *Strange But True: New York* can make a difference.

Here you will find stories of people and places, happenings, legends, myths, laws, and facts that could exist nowhere outside of Manhattan, the Bronx, Brooklyn, Queens, and Staten Island. The United States is home to some of the greatest cities in the world—San Francisco, Chicago, Washington, D.C. among them—but there is truly no greater city than New York. And no city has given rise to more that is unusual, odd, interesting, bizarre, or funny. As the author, E. B.

White wrote, "No matter where you sit in New York, you feel the vibrations of great times and tall deeds, of queer people and events and undertakings."

There are many tours of New York. Walking, gallery, and museum tours. There are backstage theatre tours. Shopping tours. Central Park tours. Harlem tours. Tours of Soho, Tribeca, Greenwich Village, Chinatown, Little Italy, Hell's Kitchen, and the Silk Stocking District. Tours to visit dead New Yorkers. But for all of these, you have to be in the city, and sometimes that's just not practical. I invite you now to join me on a special tour that you can take any time the mood hits you. Whenever you want to be amused or amazed, educated or entertained, just open a page and find yourself immersed in *Strange But True: New York*.

# PART I:
# Strange But True

No other American city is so intensely American as New York.

— Anthony Trollope, *North America*, 1862

Not only is New York City the nation's melting pot, it is also the casserole, the chafing dish, and the charcoal grill.

— John V. Lindsay, mayor of New York City, 1966–1973

Nowhere is the saying "truth is stranger than fiction" more appropriate than when describing New York and its inhabitants. No one is inventive enough to create the bizarreness that passes for life as a New Yorker. And if, as Mr. Trollope claimed, "no other American city is so intensely American as New York," then the other 49 states better beware! For all its peculiarities, however, New York City has given the world a remarkable number of buildings, institutions, and inventions that are part of the fabric of life. Some of these "gifts" are, indeed, dubious, but there is probably no other city anywhere whose people—with their diversity of background, interests, and abilities—could have thrived so freely to create so grandly. There is historical precedent for what detractors call New York's weirdness and admirers call its uniqueness. Past and present, fan or foe, New Yorkers really couldn't care less what people think, and maybe that's the strangest, or most admirable, quality of all.

## New York on Fire

Nathan Hale was hanged not only for spying, but also for trying to burn down New York City. On September 20, 1776, American soldiers from Hale's regiment, sneaked into British-held New York and stashed resin-soaked logs in buildings. A spark did the rest. Hale was caught the following day, after the fires destroyed over a quarter of the city. He was hanged without a trial because the British considered him one of the incendiaries, as well as being a spy.

## Submarine Attack

History's first submarine attack took place in New York Harbor in 1776. An inventor from Connecticut named David Bushnell developed a submarine and called it the *Turtle* because it resembled two large tortoise shells.

On September 6, 1776, the *Turtle* targeted the HMS *Eagle*, flagship of the British fleet. The submarine, with its watertight hull made of six-inch-thick oak timbers coated with tar, was supposed to secure a cache of gunpowder to the hull of the *Eagle* and sneak away before it exploded. Unfortunately, the *Turtle* got entangled with the *Eagle*'s rudder bar, lost ballast, and surfaced before the gunpowder could be planted.

## Library Lore

In its early history, the south courtyard of the New York Public Library at Fifth Avenue and 42nd Street was the scene of amateur dramatic performances, puppet shows, and at least one circus. In 1950, it took on a more mundane role when the central fountain in the courtyard's center was demolished, and the courtyard became a parking lot.

Some 530,000 cubic feet of marble was used in the construction of the library. When it opened in 1911, it was the largest marble building ever built in the United States. The marble originated from two quarries in Vermont, but over 65 percent of the stone failed to meet the architects' standards. It was rejected and used instead for other buildings, including the Harvard Medical School.

The marble floors of the library were deemed so hard that in 1911 all employees were supplied with rubber-soled shoes.

New York Public Library employees once ran a Co-operative General Store in the building's basement. The store opened in June 1920, and carried everything from stockings to sardines. It sold groceries and general merchandise, including items such as canned and fresh foodstuffs, tobacco products, clothing, and even sewing notions.

The concrete lions that guard the more than 40 million items in the library are named Patience and Fortitude.

## Public School

Erasmus Hall High School, Brooklyn, was built in 1787 as a private school for Dutch farmers' children. It is the second oldest public school in the country and the first public school building in the country to be designated a landmark.

## Ladies Pond

The Ladies Pond in Central Park was reserved for ladies-only ice skating in the 1890s. To put on skates, women had to expose their ankles, which was seen as risqué in the days when long skirts were more the norm. This would explain the need for a ladies-only pond, which would protect those sensitive, blushing ladies from any potential peeping Toms in the neighborhood. In 1936, the pond was replaced with a playground.

## Morrisania

Morrisania in the center of the Bronx was named for the family of Lewis Morris, a signatory of the Declaration of Independence.

## Herald HQ

In 1866, Broadway and Ann Street downtown was the headquarters of the *New York Herald* newspaper. It was from here that correspondent Henry Stanley was sent in March 1871 to find the missing missionary David Livingstone. Seven months later, Stanley found him at Lake Tanganyika in Africa and greeted him with the now classic phrase, "Dr. Livingstone, I presume?"

> Stanley found him at Lake Tanganyika in Africa and greeted him with the now classic phrase, "Dr. Livingstone, I presume?"

## Chambers Street Theatre

In 1844, Signor Ferdinando Palmo opened Palmo's Opera House on Chambers Street, with the intention of bringing Italian opera to New York. The venture did not work out so well and Palmo lost all his money and the theater.

It soon reopened as Burton's Chambers Street Theatre and was the first in the city to sell numbered seats, assuring late comers of having a seat. Burton's was far more popular with the public than Palmo's. Perhaps this was due to the fact that Burton's staged "artist model shows," which featured nearly naked men and women.

## Hanging Around

The site of Washington Square Park was used for burying paupers and hanging criminals from 1789 until 1823.

## Forbidden Passion in Vernon Boulevard Castle

Over 200 years ago, a French nobleman was forced to flee his native country and he ended up in Long Island City, Queens, where he built a castle with towers, secret passageways, dungeons, and gardens. After learning of the love affair between his daughter and a young worker from a lower social class, he locked them in separate dungeons.

The Vernon Boulevard Castle came into the possession of a Colonel John Bodine and for decades after was known as the Bodine Castle, a rendezvous location for New York aristocracy until it was sold to Consolidated Edison. In the mid-1960s, on the eve of the day Bodine Castle was to be designated an official New York City Landmark, Consolidated Edison demolished it.

## Slavery in New York

In the 1700s, New York was the second-largest slave-owning city in the British colonies, second only to Charleston, South Carolina. The auctioned slaves were not only African Americans but whites, dependent women, orphaned children, and debtors.

## Long Island Ferry

The first ferry to Long Island was established at around 1640 at what is now known as Dover and Pearl Streets. The passengers, the earliest recorded New York City commuters, were Dutch planters who farmed small plots in Brooklyn. The land, recently purchased from Native Americans, was still the property of the Dutch West India Company and only leased to the planters. This arrangement gave the borough its name—the word *Brjikenleen* comes from two Dutch words: *Brjiken* for "use" and *leen* for "loan."

## Crumbling Castle

Castle Garden was a fort on an artificial island about 300 feet from the mainland, and was constructed in 1807 in anticipation of the War of 1812. At the end of the war, the fort was renamed Castle Clinton in honor of DeWitt Clinton, a former mayor and later governor of New York. It was ceded to New York in 1823 and became an official greeting site. When President Andrew Jackson came there in 1833, the timber bridge from the fort to the tip of Battery Park, which was the mainland, collapsed from the weight of the president's procession, dumping a number of men and horses into the water. President Jackson had been slightly ahead of the entourage and escaped unscathed.

From 1855 until the opening of Ellis Island in 1890, Castle Clinton was the country's leading immigration depot, with seven and a half million immigrants passing through the building during that time. And from 1896 until 1941, the fort housed the city's aquarium.

## Workhouse Wares

During the 19th century, cigars and hoopskirt forms were produced at the municipal workhouse on Blackwell's Island (now Roosevelt Island).

## The Incredible Empire State Building

When the Empire State Building first opened, it was planned to be a docking port for airships. The balconies surrounding the top of the building's 16-story metal finial, now the 102nd floor, were equipped to secure and dock blimps as well as to house ticket stands and loading docks. After the building opened on May 1, 1931, and its mooring mast was declared safe, it took four months before a blimp actually moored there. It was a small, privately owned dirigible that docked for three minutes before taking flight, and this only after it had circled for 30 minutes in 40-mile-per-hour winds, to the pleasure of gawkers and the fury of traffic below. A few weeks after the September flight, a Goodyear blimp failed to dock and after a series of docking failures due to the windy conditions, the mooring tower was abandoned in favor of one purpose only: sightseeing.

## Coopering in New York

Cooperage was critical in the commercial development of New York City.

Beginning in the late 17th century, the barrel was used as a unit of measurement.

In the mid-19th century, the flour trade, sugar refineries, coffee merchants, even local distilleries, breweries, and taverns depended on the barrel method. Coopers worked near the wharves and as late as 1860, barrels were made by hand. The wood to make the

*Its importance was so crucial to the city that, to this day, two casks are depicted on the city's official seal.*

barrels came from upstate, and was floated down the Hudson and stored at docks in Brooklyn and Manhattan. In 1860, a Brooklyn cooper became one of the first in the country to employ mechanical production. There were 90 coopering firms in Manhattan and 36 in Brooklyn as late as 1900. In the years following, coopering plants moved outside the city, seeking locations closer to large forests. Pre-packaging of goods formerly sold in barrels, and the use of plastic, steel, and other materials brought an end to coopering. Its importance to the development of New York City was so crucial, however, that to this day two casks are prominently depicted on the city's official seal.

## Cowen's Inventions

Joshua Lionel Cowen was the eighth of nine children and a college dropout from both Columbia University and the City College of New York. Born in 1877, he had built his first toy train at age seven by attaching a small steam engine to a wooden locomotive he had carved. In 1898, he accidentally invented the flashlight by attaching small canisters containing batteries and light bulbs to a flower pot for the purpose of illuminating the plant. The invention was a flop so Cowen sold the rights to one Conrad Hubert who decided to try selling the lights without the flower pot. He dubbed it the Eveready Flashlight, and it's still going strong.

Cowen continued his interest in trains. He sold his first electric train in 1901 to a store owner in Manhattan and the Lionel Corporation was in business. It was Cowen's skills as a marketer that truly put toy trains on the map. In the 1920s, it was he who convinced owners of large department stores to incorporate elaborate train setups around their large Christmas tree displays. For a short time in the early 1950s, Lionel was the largest toy manufacturer in the world. Cowen died in 1965.

## Origins of A & P

In 1859, the intersection of Church Street and Vesey Street was part of the wharf district where two men George Hartford and George Gillman began their small tea company, which sold tea directly from the ships to their New York City customers. Eventually, this became the Great Atlantic and Pacific Tea Company, better known as A & P, one of the largest companies in the world.

## Coney Island

In 1824, the Terhune brothers opened the Coney Island House in southwestern Brooklyn. After the Civil War, five railroads were constructed that connected Coney Island with the rest of Brooklyn, and that's when it really began to thrive. The island got its name from the Dutch word "*konijn*," meaning rabbit, because there were so many wild rabbits in the area. Henry Hudson came across the island the day before discovering the land where the colony of New Amsterdam was eventually founded. Coney Island has six miles of beach and its boardwalk is two miles long.

> Feltman's competitors started the rumor that his sausages contained dog meat, thus coining the now familiar term "hot dog."

In 1852, the butchers' guild in Frankfurt, Germany, introduced a sausage that was spiced, smoked, and packed in a thin, almost transparent casing. Its origin gave rise to the word "frankfurter." In 1867, the German-American immigrant Charles Feltman started selling these sausages from his pie pushcart at Coney Island. Feltman's competitors started the false rumor that his sausages contained dog meat, thus coining the now familiar term "hot dog."

As business boomed, Feltman hired a young man, Nathan Handwerker, as a part-time delivery boy. It didn't take long before Nathan progressed to owning his own hot dog stand. He did so well that today, Nathan's is a fast-food chain that produces packaged frankfurters to be sold in grocery stores throughout the United States.

Roller coasters, public bathing, and carousels appeared in Coney Island in 1884, followed by horse races, boxing matches, dance halls, brothels, and gambling dens. By 1907, visitors on an average weekend would mail 250,000 postcards from Coney Island.

The Polar Bear Club at Coney Island was founded in 1903 and still has 50 regular members who swim on the first day of each year, regardless of the freezing water temperatures. To be eligible to join, a potential candidate for membership of the club must undergo a body-numbing, grand total of 15 swims between November and May.

## Revolutionary War

The first engagement of the Continental and British armies in the Revolutionary War was the Battle of Brooklyn in August 1776. It was also the war's largest battle.

## Woodhull's Women

In the winter of 1870, Victoria C. Woodhull, the suffragette, opened the country's first brokerage firm operated by women with her long-time patron, Cornelius Vanderbilt. He was a client from Woodhull's earlier career as a clairvoyant.

## Woolworths

In 1872, F. W. Woolworth's "five-and-dime" stores introduced the concept of shopping for fun and just browsing. Before this, merchandise was not on display. Customers would enter a store knowing exactly what they wanted and could bargain over the price.

## Animal Magic

The first rhinoceros ever exhibited in America was seen at Peale's Museum and Gallery of the Fine Arts on Broadway in 1826. The first giraffes in America were shown at a vacant lot on lower Broadway in 1838. The two giraffes were the only ones who had survived out of the original eleven brought over from southern Africa.

## Kennel Club

In 1876, a group of dog lovers met at the Westminster Hotel on East 16th Street and Irving Place, and formed the Westminster Kennel Club. The Westminster

Show is second only to the Kentucky Derby as the oldest continuous sporting event in America.

## Marxists in Manhattan

In 1857, at 148 Fulton Street, Joseph Wedemeyer, a friend of Karl Marx and Friedrich Engels, founded the Communist Club of New York, the first Marxist organization in the Western Hemisphere.

## Lighting Up the City

In 1880, the electric streetlight first appeared in New York City at Broadway and 23rd Street. It illuminated an advertisement for homes on Long Island and was manually turned off each night at 11 P.M.

*Edison turned the switch...to illuminate Broad and Wall streets for the first time with 106 electric lamps.*

At the same time, Thomas Edison was perfecting the light bulb for use at home and in stores. On September 4, 1882, Edison turned the switch at the offices of J. P. Morgan & Co., one of his wealthiest clients, to illuminate Broad and Wall Streets for the first time with 106 electric lamps.

## Cherokee Club

At the beginning of the 20th century, a clubhouse known as the Cherokee Club was built on the Upper East Side of Manhattan. It was a branch of the powerful Democratic patronage powerbrokers of Tammany Hall, and featured a big portrait of Boss Tweed, and two giant bas-relief Indian heads above the doorway. Efforts to make the club a landmark failed, and the clubhouse itself was demolished. Today, the neighborhood is known as Cherokee Place and other buildings have incorporated the name, including the local Cherokee Post Office and the Cherokee Apartments.

## City of Learning

New York City contains world-renowned universities including Columbia University and New York University, but in 1898, it was the last American city of that time to open public schools.

## 75 Bedford Street

75 Bedford Street in Greenwich Village was the home of poet Edna St. Vincent Millay and is the narrowest house in the city at only nine feet wide.

# Why is New York City called the Big Apple?

The term "Big Apple" was first used by author Edward S. Martin in his 1909 book, *The Wayfarer in New York*, to reflect the sentiment that the city received more than a fair share of the nation's wealth. The Big Apple was popularized in the 1920s by John J. Fitzgerald, a sportswriter for the *Morning Telegraph*, a New York City newspaper. Fitzgerald had overheard stable hands in New Orleans refer to New York City's racetracks as "the Big Apple." He named his racing column, "Around the Big Apple," and once wrote: "The Big Apple. The dream of every lad that ever threw a leg over a thoroughbred and the goal of all horsemen. There's only one Big Apple. That's New York." Then, in the 1930s, jazz musicians adopted the term as a way of saying, "There are many apples on the success tree, but when you play in New York City, you play the Big Apple."

## Black Tom Blasts

On July 30, 1916, the Black Tom Island explosions occurred at the United Express Building on Rector Street, breaking 425 plate glass windows. The explosions were heard as far away as Maryland. Black Tom Island was a manmade peninsula along the New Jersey shore in the New York Harbor, where more than two million pounds of munitions bound for wartime England and France were stored. It was not until 1939 that it was proven the explosions had been an act of German espionage—prior to America's entry into World War I. Seven people were killed.

## Dangerous Driving

The nation's first automobile accident occurred in New York City in 1897 when the speed limit was nine miles an hour. The nation's first auto-fatality occurred three years later. Nothing much has changed in the intervening years—driving in New York may still be hazardous to one's health.

## Big Yellow Taxi

Why are New York cabs yellow? The man who founded the Yellow Cab Company in 1907 chose the color, after reading a study conducted by the University of Chicago, because it is the easiest color to spot. Regardless of how bright the color, however, getting a cab in New York will never be considered easy.

## 23 Skiddoo

The Flatiron Building on 23rd Street and Fifth Avenue was one of the first sky-scrapers built. One of the unfortunate side effects of its design was that its triangular shape produced wind currents, causing women's skirts to blow up. The police in the area created the term "23 skiddoo" to shoo gapers from the area.

## Secret Subway

On the corner of Broadway and Warren Street was a building whose basement contained the hidden entrance to a subterranean room. Furnished with a grand piano, fountain, and goldfish tank, it was actually the waiting room and ticket office for New York's earliest subway. Alfred Ely Beach, publisher of *Scientific American,* invented and secretly built the project that comprised a tunnel 12 feet below Broadway. Opened to the public in 1870, it was designed for compressed air propulsion and was nine feet in diameter. Over the following year, 400,000 people rode the car for 25 cents a ride, the proceeds going to charity. This type of subway system turned out to be too expensive to produce, so instead Beach rented out the tunnel as a shooting gallery and wine cellar.

## Kosher Meat

Asser Levy was New York's first kosher butcher. He came to New Amsterdam in 1654.

## Walter in Waverly

The name Waverly Place in Washington Square honors Sir Walter Scott, author of 32 Waverly novels.

## Bonaparte's Hideaway

In the mid-1800s, Joseph Bonaparte, Napoleon's nephew, built several sprawling houses in New York City to hold his uncle's extensive art collection and to serve as a possible refuge for him.

## Elizabeth Arden

Elizabeth Arden, born Florence Nightingale Graham in Ontario, Canada, moved to New York City when she was 30. In two years, she opened a beauty salon and changed her name. She was the first person to introduce mascara into the United States and the first to employ saleswomen as traveling demonstrators.

## Cable Railway

The first commercial passenger cable railway in the United States ran on the world's first elevated line, on Greenwich Street and 9th Avenue in Manhattan from 1868 until steam locomotives were introduced there in 1871.

## Cathedral Church of St. John

The world's largest gothic cathedral is the Cathedral Church of St. John the Divine at West 112th Street in the Morningside Heights section of Manhattan. It was begun in 1892 as a Romanesque design and converted in 1911 to the gothic style. Its nave, the longest is the world, is 601 feet.

## Temple Emanu-El

The world's largest synagogue is Temple Emanu-El in Manhattan.

## St. Patrick's Cathedral

St. Patrick's Cathedral, originally located on Mott Street, opened in 1815 as the city's first Catholic church. Now on Fifth Avenue, it is the largest Catholic church in the United States. It seats 2,500 and there are 7,300 pipes in its pipe organ. Its rose stained-glass window measures 26 feet across and its two spires are each 300 feet high.

## Grand Central

There are six windows in Grand Central Terminal, each with 600 panes of glass.

## Bronx Zoo

The Bronx Zoo opened in 1899, but was founded in 1895 as the New York Zoological Society and did not have its first natural habitats until 1941. Today, the Bronx Zoo is the largest metropolitan wildlife park in the United States.

## New York Nuggets

There are 2,000 bridges in New York City and 6,400 miles of streets.

### Halloween

The nation's largest public Halloween parade takes place in Greenwich Village.

### Times Traffic

Nearly 37 million people visit Times Square each year.

### Bike New York

Held the first Sunday in May, the 42-mile Bike New York Tour visits all five boroughs of New York City, making it the longest event of its kind in the United States.

### World's Largest Clock

The world's largest clock sits atop the Williamsburgh Savings Bank in Brooklyn. Each of the clock's four sides has a diameter of 27 feet.

## Stock Exchange

The New York Stock Exchange is the world's largest, and has an annual trading volume of $5.5 trillion. It began in 1792 when 24 brokers met under a buttonwood tree facing 68 Wall Street.

## Macy's

Macy's is the world's largest store, covering 2.1 million square feet and stocking over 500,000 different items.

## New York in Scale

The Panorama of the City of New York in the Queens Museum of Art is the world's largest architectural model, containing 895,000 individual structures at a scale of 1 inch equals 100 feet.

## Oldest Golf Course

The oldest municipal golf course in the country was opened in 1895 and is in Van Cortlandt Park in the Bronx.

## First Brewery

The first public brewery in America was opened in Manhattan in 1633 in the Market Field, which is now the financial district. Colonists loved their beer and often had a mug of it with breakfast.

## Oldest Canoe Club

The oldest canoe club in the country is the New York Canoe Club, established in 1871.

## Academy of Dramatic Arts

The American Academy of Dramatic Arts is the oldest acting school in the English-speaking world. Founded in New York City in 1884, it was attended by such eventual thespian stars as Lauren Bacall, Kirk Douglas, and Spencer Tracy.

## Pig Mania

As late as the 1840s, thousands of pigs roamed Manhattan to consume garbage—the city's first sanitation system.

## Early Skyscraper

In 1664, the city's tallest structure was a two-story windmill.

## Voorlezer's House

The oldest schoolhouse still standing in America, built in 1695, is situated in Historic Richmond Town on Staten Island; it is called Voorlezer's House.

## School for the Blind

The nation's first school for blind children opened in 1833 as a result of the spread of conjunctivitis in the almshouses that left many children blind.

## Church for the Deaf

The world's first church for those with speech and hearing impairments is St. Ann's in Washington Heights.

## Floyd Bennett Field

The city's first airport was Floyd Bennett Field in Brooklyn, named after Floyd Bennett who flew Admiral Byrd across the North Pole in 1926.

## Gotham City

New York City is often referred to as Gotham which means "goat town" and came to refer to New York when Washington Irving used it satirically in his 1807 series *Salmagundi: or, the Whim-whams and Opinions of Launcelot Langstaff and Others*. Gotham was a town in England noted for its "wise

> New York is often referred to as Gotham which means "goat town." Gotham was a town known for its "wise fools."

fools," which led to the saying, "More fools pass through Gotham than remain in it." The residents of Gotham in England wanted to discourage people from settling in their town so they purposely acted insane whenever strangers visited. Irving thought New Yorkers had adopted the same strategy.

## Sheep Meadow

For 70 years, from 1864 to 1934, sheep resided in the 22-acre area of Central Park between 66th and 69th street, now called the Sheep Meadow. The sheep were moved to Prospect Park in Brooklyn in 1934.

## New Yorkers at the Alamo

In 1836, approximately 187 Texan revolutionaries died at the Alamo in San Antonio. Eight of them were from New York. General Santa Anna, commander of the Mexican forces at the Alamo, was later overthrown from his dictatorship and exiled from Mexico to Staten Island.

## Maiden Lane

Maiden Lane in the Financial District was named for women who washed clothes for a living.

## Featherbed Lane

Featherbed Lane is an extremely curvy street in the Bronx. Appropriately, the name came from the 1840s when the street was lined with brothels. At that time, immigrants were coming to the area, notably Irish people, and Featherbed Lane was given as a nickname for the red-light district that quickly sprang up.

## Liquid City

In 1885, there were 10,000 drinking establishments in New York City, one for every 140 residents.

## Philip Morris Company

In 1902, Philip Morris, a British tobacco and food processor company, opened its first American branch in New York City on Broad Street. In 1955, it introduced the "Marlboro Man." It is the largest industrial corporation in New York City.

## Women's Hotel

The Martha Washington Hotel opened in 1903 and was the first hotel in the United States exclusively for women.

## Wall Street Explosion

In 1913, J. P. Morgan & Company built their bank's headquarters in a building of white marble at 23 Wall Street. One side of the building is pockmarked. On September 16, 1920, a driver parked his horse-drawn cart next to the bank during lunch hour, before mysteriously disappearing. The cart was filled with dynamite and it exploded, killing 33 people and the horse, injuring 400 people, and scarring the side of the building. The driver was never found.

## Brother Islands

North Brother Island is an island in the East River at the entrance to Long Island Sound and is part of the Bronx. Its neighbor island is called South Brother Island, and the Dutch named both of them the Gezellen or companions. In 1885, the city built Riverside Hospital on North Brother Island for the treatment of infectious diseases. The best-known patient was Typhoid Mary (Mary Mallon) who was institutionalized there from 1915 until her death in 1938.

## 21 Club

In 1922, the 21 Club, a restaurant located in three connecting brownstones, was founded in Greenwich Village, but then moved to West 52nd Street on New Year's Eve in 1929. It was raided once in 1930 during Prohibition, and the result was the construction of a secret wine cellar still used today. During Prohibition, there were 38 speakeasies on West 52nd Street.

## Oh, Christmas Tree

The first Christmas tree was plugged in at Rockefeller Plaza in 1933. Since then five miles of Christmas lights are used on each tree every year. On January 8, the tree is taken down and ground into mulch to be used as ground cover at a Boy Scout camp in New Jersey.

## The Circus Comes to Town

New York City was a favored destination of circus acts. A live lion was exhibited there as early as 1728. In the decades after the American Revolution, the city was one of few in the United States where leisure pursuits were not prohibited for moral reasons. The first circus was Englishman John Bill Ricketts', which ran for four months in 1793 and returned five more times in the next several years. An elephant, the first in the country, was exhibited in Manhattan in 1796.

Exhibitions were mounted several times between 1808 and 1813 by a team of Europeans, and then between 1817 and 1822 by the Englishman James West. Seeking to eliminate competition from West, two theatrical producers bought him out and engaged the first bareback rider, James Hunter, who made his debut in New York City in 1823.

In New York City, various theatres, exhibition halls, and vacant lots were sites of one-ring circuses. In 1843 and 1854, a huge building called the Hippodrome opened at Broadway and 23rd Street and took up two acres. Here circus acts competed with races that could include chariots, ostriches, and ponies ridden by monkeys.

In 1881, P. T. Barnum merged with James A. Bailey's circus to form the first three-ring circus which made its debut at Madison Square Garden (then located between Madison and 4th avenues at 26th and 27th streets).

*The present in New York is so powerful that the past is lost.*

— John Jay Chapman in a letter from 1898

## Slave Remains

In 1991, more than 400 remains of what is believed to be the first group of African slaves brought to the city over two hundred years before were discovered by construction workers. The first black settlers came in 1626; they were 12 Angolan men and were not slaves.

## Natural Manhattan

Manhattan's southern tip, what is usually referred to as downtown, is mostly landfill. "Natural" Manhattan, land that was not constructed by artificial means, makes up only 75 percent of the total downtown area.

## On Broadway

Broadway began as an Algonquin Indian trade route called the Wiechquaekeck Trail. Originating from lower Manhattan at Bowling Green and ending in Albany, it is one of the world's longest streets and totals 150 miles. Its official name is Highway 9.

## Green-Wood Cemetery

Green-Wood Cemetery in Brooklyn's Sunset Park boasts a spectacular harbor view and 478 acres of trees and flowering shrubs. However, the notables interred there, including Leonard Bernstein, "Boss" Tweed, and F.A.O. Schwartz, cannot take advantage of the setting.

## Native New Yorker

There are about 30,000 Native Americans living in New York City.

## A Bite of the Apple

Manhattan contains only 20 percent of New York City's population.

## Computer Literate

In 1986, the School of Visual Arts, New York, became the first accredited college in the United States to offer a bachelor of fine arts degree in computer arts.

## Aerial Trams

The Roosevelt Island Tram opened in 1976 to transport commuters from the mainland of Manhattan back and forth to Roosevelt Island, when it became residential. It is the only aerial commuter tram in the United States.

## Pure Gold

The Federal Reserve Bank of New York is the largest of the 12 banks in the Federal Reserve System, and functions as the banker for the entire U.S. government. The branch in New York City handles all foreign exchange trading and holds gold from 80 countries and organizations that, at the end of the 20th century, was valued at $117 billion, making it the world's largest store of gold. The gold held at Fort Knox is worth about half as much.

## All That Glitters

Approximately 40 percent of the world's monetary gold is stored in New York City, five stories underground in a vault that is 76 feet below the street, 50 feet below sea level, and accessible only by special elevator. Twelve thousand tons of gold are held in 122 cells. Each gold brick weighs 27 pounds and there are over 700,000 bricks in the bank. Security can seal off the entire building within 30 seconds. When one country pays a debt to another, the gold is not shipped from country to country, but rather moved only from cell to cell.

## Television Takes Hold

In 1926, the National Broadcasting Company was founded in New York City as the nation's first coast-to-coast network. Businessmen representing the Radio Corporation of America, General Electric, and Westinghouse were the principals.

In 1939, President Franklin D. Roosevelt became the first president to appear on television, broadcasting from the New York World's Fair.

## Park Plans

Central Park was conceived and planned in the parlor of the townhouse owned by Calvert Vaux, a landscape designer who, with his friend and partner, Frederick Law Olmstead, mapped out their design for the park. The team's winning design, called the "Greensward Plan," almost missed the April 1, 1858 deadline and was the last entrant submitted to the judges.

In Central Park, there is a statue of Balto, the lead sled dog who transported diphtheria serum across Alaska in the winter of 1825.

There are 125 drinking fountains in Central Park. On any given day, it is doubtful if even 20 work.

There are 40 ornate bridges in Central Park. One of them, Greywacke Arch, is named for the variety of sandstone with which it is built.

Ramble Arch at five feet wide is the narrowest in Central Park. The Ramble is the center of birding in New York City with 230 species having been spotted over the years. There's a tumbling stream called "The Gill" which is totally artificial and manmade, turned on and off with a water tap.

The Ramble is home to Indian Cave which is a naturally occurring rock cleft with a slab of stone set over the top by Olmstead and Vaux. The cleft was sealed at both ends in the 1930s. Also known as the Sea Cave, it was actually created long after Indians left the area, and became home only to tramps.

## Consequences of the Revolution

During the American Revolution, New York City was the primary location for detaining prisoners of war. They were held in public buildings, old warehouses, and on 11 infamous prison ships. An estimated 11,000 revolutionaries died on these ships.

## Bronx Beauty

The Bronx has the largest amount of park acreage in New York City. Two of the parks, Van Cortlandt Park and Pelham Bay Park, combined have 3,800 acres, and much of the parks are undeveloped and wild. To this day, foxes, coyotes, and wild turkeys can be found there.

## Pines for Purchase

The first retail Christmas tree lot in the United States was opened in 1851 in New York City.

# A River Runs Through It

The East River is not actually a river. Technically, a river is a stream of fresh water that empties into another body of water. The East River is basically an arm of the sea, known as a tidal estuary, that is fed by the Atlantic Ocean through Long Island Sound and through New York Harbor. Further proof that East River is not a river is that the East River's current changes directions; rivers, on the other hand, do not do this.

## Crystal District

New York's Crystal District, five blocks along Madison Avenue between 58th and 63rd streets, houses more luxury crystal outlets than any other quarter-mile of real estate in the world.

## Chinatown

New York City's Chinatown is the largest Chinatown in the United States with a population estimated at between 70,000 and 150,000.

## New York Post

The New York Post is the oldest running newspaper in the country. It was established in 1803 by Alexander Hamilton.

## Steam-Powered Elevator

The world's first passenger elevator was installed in the five-story Haughwout Building on Broadway by Elisha Graves Otis. It was steam-powered, rose 40 feet a minute, and cost $300 to build. The elevator operated for 50 years.

The world's first hotel with an elevator was The Fifth Avenue, opened in New York City in 1859.

> The world's first passenger elevator...was steam-powered, rose 40 feet a minute, and cost $300 to build.

## Bellevue Hospital

Bellevue Hospital, established in 1734, is the oldest general hospital in North America. In 1869, it was the first in the country to offer a hospital-based ambulance service, and in 1873, it established the country's first nursing school.

## The Strand

If you put the books from The Strand, the world's largest secondhand bookstore, end to end they would stretch eight miles.

## Natural History Museum

The American Museum of Natural History in Manhattan is the largest natural history museum in the world, with over 36 million artifacts.

## Watch Your Step

A single stretch of Manhattan sidewalk has more dog poop per inch than manure on an Idaho cornfield on Planting Day.

## Hot in the City

The surface temperature of an average New York City street during a hot summer day is 150 degrees Fahrenheit. An egg begins to cook at 145 degrees Fahrenheit.

## Too Close for Comfort

Manhattan has the highest population density in North America.

## Designer Labels

The most commercially expensive street in the world is Fifth Avenue from 49th to 57th streets.

## Going Underground

There are 722 miles of subway track and 6,374.6 miles of streets. The subway trains stop at 469 stations.

## Commercial Clout

The first television commercial was a 20-second ad for a Bulova clock, broadcast in New York during a baseball game between the Brooklyn Dodgers and the Philadelphia Phillies. Bulova paid $9 for the spot.

## The Cloisters

The Cloisters, a branch of the Metropolitan Museum of Art, is the only museum in America dedicated exclusively to medieval art.

## Checkmate

The first American chess tournament was held in New York in 1843.

## Lady Liberty

The Statue of Liberty has a 35-foot waist and an eight-foot index finger. Her nose is 53 inches long, and her ears are so big at 3.3 feet each that workers sat inside them during construction.

## Statue Statistics

History has it that the sculptor of the Statue of Liberty, Frenchman Bartholdi, modeled the face after his mother and the body after his mistress. So very French!

Liberty Island used to be called Bedloes Island and was used to house a gallows.

## King Kullen

Instead of being served by a store owner, customers helped themselves to groceries in the store established by Michael Kullen in 1930. This is why it is considered to be the first grocery store in the country. The store opened in Queens and was so successful that it was the start of the King Kullen grocery chain.

## Suspend Your Belief

The longest suspension bridge in the country is the Verrazano-Narrows Bridge, which is 4,260 feet long and connects Brooklyn and Staten Island. The towers were deliberately constructed so that they were not exactly parallel but a few inches out to accommodate the curvature of the earth.

*It is a miracle that New York works at all. The whole thing is implausible.*

— E. B. White, *Here is New York*, 1948

## Wooden Wall Street

From 1653 to 1699, a wooden wall stood on what is now Wall Street. The wall was built by the Dutch to protect the city against attack from American Indians and the British. Its strength as a means of protection was never tested. It has lasted, however, as the universal symbol of the financial world.

## Children's Museum

The Brooklyn Children's Museum is the world's first museum for youngsters.

## History of Staten Island

Staten Island, also known as Richmond County, was originally discovered by 16th-century Italian explorer Giovanni da Verrazano. In 1687, the Duke of York offered it as a prize to the winner of a sailing race.

## Saint in the City

Mother Cabrini became America's first canonized saint in 1946. She is visible in the altar at St. Frances Xavier Cabrini Chapel, at Mother Cabrini High School in the Bronx. Hers is the only actual saint's body in the world displayed in its entirety, except for the head which has been replaced with a wax replica. Her real head is in Italy.

## Manhattan Mausoleum

The General Grant National Memorial in Riverside Park and 122nd Street is the largest mausoleum in the United States. It is the burial site of Ulysses and Julia Grant.

## Luxury Lunching

Delmonico's was the first luxury restaurant in New York City, founded by Swiss immigrants who ran it from 1835–1881. It was here that culinary classics such as eggs benedict, lobster Newburg, and the Delmonico steak were created.

## Lincoln Center

Lincoln Center for the Performing Arts was America's first performing arts center; it opened in 1962.

## Masked Money Making

In 1899, New York City's coffers increased by $38,000 as a result of issuing permits for masquerade balls.

## Hell's Gate

Randall's Island and Ward's Island are in the East and Harlem Rivers, and are connected by a footbridge. Together, they make up a total of 500 acres that house the Fire Department Academy as well as over 300 people at the homeless shelter and psychiatric center located there. Hell's Gate is the name given to a turbulent channel where the East and Harlem Rivers meet between Astoria, Queens, and Ward's Island.

## City Island

City Island is a small community at the edge of New York City located in the Bronx. Originally inhabited by the Siwanoy Indians, who lived on the clams, oysters, and fish that were in plentiful supply there, it was first established as an English settleiment in 1685.

It has a rich nautical history because of its strategic location between Manhattan and points north. It became an important shipping and ship building center during the 18th and 19th centuries and five America's Cup winners have been built in its boatyards.

## Governor's Island

Governor's Island is located at Main Street and Early Bird Road off the tip of Manhattan in New York Harbor. The Dutch bought the island from the Indians in

1637 for two axes and some nails, and ever since, no one has known what to do with it. Originally it was called Nuttin Island because of the nut, oak, and hickory trees that flourished there. When the then governor of New York, Wouter Van Twiller,

> The Dutch bought the island from the Indians in 1637 for two axes and some nails...

bought the island, the name changed to Governor's Island. In 1812, it became a permanent military base, and then in 1966, it was handed over to the Coast Guard who couldn't afford to keep it open. Now it belongs officially to the City of New York, who doesn't know what to do with it, either. There are tours to see Castle William and Fort Jay, both intact from the island's days as a military base.

## Greedy Governor

Wouter Van Twiller was the fifth director general or governor of New Netherland and ruled from 1633 through 1637. He is credited with being the first public official to corrupt political office for personal gain. As governor, he deeded to himself several hundred acres of prime tobacco farmland, bought three islands, a share in 15,000 acres in Brooklyn, and a similar amount of land on Long Island.

# New Year's Eve at Times Square

Long before throngs filled Times Square to watch the ball drop on New Year's Eve, the bells of Lower Manhattan's Trinity Church would ring in the new year. In 1894, believing that the din from the crowds gathered around the tower had grown too great and disruptive, Rector Morgan Dix ordered the bell-ringing to stop. In 1902, *The New York Times* moved their offices from Lower Manhattan to what was then called Longacre Square in midtown. In 1904, the name of the area was changed to Times Square, and on December 31, 1904, the *Times* set off a spectacular fireworks display above its new building. Then, on December 31, 1907 a sphere surrounded with electric lights was lowered from the top of the Times Tower office building by rope, and the New Year's Eve tradition of the lowering of the ball began.

## Trinity Church

Trinity Church's ornate 281-foot stone spire made it the highest structure in Manhattan from 1846 until the Brooklyn Bridge opened 30 years later. The churchyard is the final resting place for Robert Fulton, Alexander Hamilton, and Francis Lewis, the only signatory of the Declaration of Independence who is buried in Manhattan. The churchyard also contains the nation's first tomb to unknown soldiers, known as the Martyr's Monument. It was built to honor unidentified colonial soldiers who died in British prisons in the city during the American Revolution.

## Riverside Church

The 1930 gothic Riverside Church at 120th Street and Riverside Drive features an observation deck and the world's largest set of carillon bells.

## Island of Immigration

Ellis Island was New York's main immigration station from 1892–1954 and more than 12 million people passed through its system. The doctors' initial examination of each immigrant only lasted six seconds. If further investigation was deemed necessary, the immigrants' clothes were marked with chalk.

## Football Facts

At least five New York Yankee teams were football teams and played in the Bronx in Yankee Stadium. In the inaugural season in 1926, the team included football legend, Red Grange, also known as the Galloping Ghost for his speed as a running back. Yankee teams played in 1936, 1937, and 1940 under two different American Football Leagues. Any new league that hoped to challenge the National Football League established a team to play in Yankee Stadium hoping that some of the baseball's team winning ways would rub off on the football field.

In 1946, the brand new All-American Football Conference was created and included a New York Yankee team. There was even a Brooklyn Dodgers football team; both teams folded at the end of that season when the National Football League absorbed the league. Then in 1950, the NFL had a team called the New York Bulldogs which became the Yanks, but was disbanded after two seasons.

During the Depression, from 1929 to 1932, there was the Staten Island Stapletons, members of the National Football League. The team was taken over by the Stapleton Athletic Club after its Brooklyn's owner dissolved the franchise.

## The Construction of Brooklyn Bridge

The Brooklyn Bridge was the first steel suspension bridge ever built. It opened in 1883, and was responsible for between 20 and 30 deaths, including the designer John Roebling who died of tetanus poisoning after being knocked off a pier in 1869. His son took over the project but then succumbed to the bends while working on the excavation and afterward, supervised the operation with a telescope from his sick room. Twelve pedestrians were trampled during the opening ceremony, when there was panic after someone said the bridge was collapsing.

## Brooklyn—The Bigger Apple

Brooklyn is more populous than Manhattan with over 2.3 million people living there and "only" 1.5 million in Manhattan.

## Topps Gum Company

In 1938 the Topps Chewing Gum Company was formed to manufacture baseball cards and chewing gum called Bazooka.

## Mr. Peanut

Times Square used to be home to a real, live Mr. Peanut who was an employee of the Planter's Peanut store on Broadway. The store had a brilliant, 15,000-bulb Mr. Peanut sign, and the store was the largest in a national chain. The live Mr. Peanut wore white spats, cuffs, and gloves, carried a black cane, had a hard plastic peanut "shell" for his body and a top hat. He would wander up and down Broadway in front of the Planter's store, pointing to the store with his cane and occasionally giving away free bags of peanuts.

## Nights at the Casino

Some people think there used to be a casino in Central Park, but in fact it was a very fancy restaurant, called the Casino, located where Central Park's famous Summerstage now exists. The restaurant was built in 1846 by Calvert Vaux, one of the designers of Central Park, and it was intended as a ladies refreshment salon. Then, in the early 1920s, the restaurant became a "quiet little night club," which seems like an oxymoron, especially considering that the Casino was a favorite hangout of James Walker, New York City's flamboyant mayor. The club had a silver and maroon dining room, a glass-walled ballroom, and an orchestra that would play Walker's theme song, "Will You Love Me in December?" whenever he walked into the room.

The park's commissioner at that time was Robert Moses and there was bad blood between him and the mayor. Moses believed the prices at the Casino were too high and that it only catered for the likes of the mayor's cronies and power brokers and should be removed from Central Park. The park was supposed to provide free entertainment for all the citizens. Ultimately, after a series of suits and countersuits, the New York State Appeals Court ruled in favor of the park's commissioner. Twenty-four hours later, amid the pounding of jackhammers and a cloud of dust, the Casino was totally demolished.

## Hit the Home Run

Babe Ruth hit the first home run in Yankee Stadium in the first game ever played there in 1932.

## Tree of Hope

There used to be a tree on the center island of Seventh Avenue and 131st Street in Harlem called the "tree of hope." The tree was located across from the Lafayette Theatre which was built in 1910. For the next 30 years, this was the nation's leading black theater. Entertainers who fell on hard times performed in front of the tree, believing it had the power to bring good luck. Urban renewal took care of the original tree as well as the two that followed, but the tree still serves as inspiration. Its stump is a fixture on the stage of the Apollo Theatre on West 125th Street, and wannabe stars rub it for luck.

## Campbell's Italian Villa

In the 1920s, a tycoon named John W. Campbell had an office and a duplex apartment modeled after an Italian villa constructed above Grand Central Terminal's southwest corner. It is still in existence today, with a two-story ceiling, walnut paneling, oak floors, and leaded-glass windows, and functions as a popular bar and restaurant for commuters and others. At one time, the hideaway was headquarters for Metro-North's police department. Above the terminal's main waiting room are two tennis courts that did not belong to Campbell. Today they still exist as the Tennis Club, leased by the Trump Organization.

# The Host of the Waldorf-Astoria

Oscar Tschirky was the maître d'hôtel at the Waldorf-Astoria Hotel. He introduced to the restaurant a salad that consisted of just three ingredients: cubed apples, chopped celery, and mayonnaise. Although he was not a cook, the salad was credited as being his invention and became known as the Waldorf salad. Tschirky was born in Switzerland in 1866, and came to New York with his mother in 1883. He immediately went to work as a busboy at a restaurant off Madison Avenue, but decided that wasn't his thing, especially after spotting Lillian Russell dining at the nearby Delmonico's. He fell madly in love with her, and soon was working as a waiter at the restaurant. In less than ten years, he was hired as the headwaiter at the Waldorf. His only letter of recommendation was signed by Diamond Jim Brady and Lillian Russell. Tschirky became known as the Host of the Waldorf-Astoria, considered in the upper echelon of management right behind the manager, treasurer, and president. Today, there is a restaurant named for him at the hotel.

## It's in the Mail

A woman from Brooklyn was vacationing in New Jersey 37 years ago. She put a postcard in the mail to her mother in Pennsylvania who called her only recently to thank her for the card. It turned out that the card had two postmarks: one marked August 19, 1967 when the woman had been in New Jersey and one marked July 14, 2004 from Brooklyn, New York. The postcard had slipped behind a machine that was only recently moved and so finally discovered. It was a person in the U.S. Post Office undelivered mail unit in Brooklyn that added postage and the zip code, which had not existed 37 years ago.

## Subway Great

Marilyn Monroe's famous "white dress" scene in the movie, *The Seven Year Itch*, was filmed over a subway grate in front of the Loews New York Hotel on Lexington Avenue and 51st Street.

## Coin Collector

A man regularly cleans the reflecting pool in the plaza in front of the Vivian Beaumont Theatre in Lincoln Center, sweeping up all the coins people throw in. The fountain and pool are cleaned, drained, and swept every two months. The money collected—usually pennies—amounts to between $50 and $100. The coins are cleaned and deposited directly into an account used for the maintenance and upkeep of the fountain and plaza.

## Turkish Delight

The country's first Turkish bath opened in Brooklyn in 1863.

## Uncovered Genius

Zora Neale Hurston, a bestselling author today, died in poverty in 1960, her novels unpublished, her grave unmarked. One of her unpublished folklore manuscripts gathered dust for 30 years in a basement at Columbia University in a file that once belonged to a professor of anthropology. The files were then moved to the Smithsonian Institution in Washington, D.C., where they languished for another 20 years until anything with Zora Neale Hurston's name on it was finally recognized as important. New York publisher HarperCollins finally published the manuscript, a collection of black southern folk tales.

## Manhattan Transfer

Manhattan Transfer was the name of an interchange station in the Meadowlands in New Jersey where passengers could change between trains to or from Pennsylvania Station in New York. The transfer station is now defunct but lives on as the title of a novel by John Dos Passos, as well as the name of a popular singing group.

## The Night Before Christmas

The original itinerary of St. Nicholas and his reindeer was conceived by New York poet and scholar of ancient Hebrew, Clement Clarke Moore, in *The Night Before Christmas*. He grew up in a mansion south of what is now 23rd Street, and wrote the poem in 1823 as an entertainment for his children. A copy made its way to the *Troy Sentinel* where it was published on December 23, 1823, although Moore was not acknowledged as the writer until 1837.

A generous and wealthy man, Moore donated the site for what became the General Theological Seminary, where he became the first professor of Greek, Hebrew, and Oriental languages. He also divided his estate into lots for development and the area eventually became known as Chelsea. Moore is buried in Trinity Cemetery in Washington Heights.

## Circle Line

Circle Line sightseeing boats travel around Manhattan counterclockwise because of a tricky bit of navigation at Manhattan's northwestern tip known as Spuyten Duyvil Creek which opens into a rushing body of water. Spuyten Duyvil is Dutch in origin, and one translation is "Devil's whirlpool" while another translation is "to spite the Devil." It runs from the Hudson River to the Harlem River, and is also known as the Harlem River Ship Canal.

# PART II:
# Law & Disorder

*I love New York City; I've got a gun.*

— Charles Barkley, National Basketball Association
superstar with the Philadelphia 76ers

*In New York City we need police officers to protect even the dead.*

— William J. Dean, *Time* magazine, 1983

From the beginning, New York and New Yorkers were never considered lawless. That was a term reserved for cowboys and gunslingers in the Old West, but New York? No, not lawless. Not particularly law-abiding, either, though. New York's provincialism extends to rules and regulations: there is the rest of the world's and then there is New York's. That is not to say that over the centuries, sheriffs, detectives, patrolmen, and police commissioners—including the redoubtable Theodore Roosevelt, the city's first police commissioner—have not instituted a veritable encyclopedia of laws to help New Yorkers live with respect for their property and their neighbors and to protect them, often from themselves. But as has already been illustrated, New Yorkers do not take kindly to being told what to do, even when it's for their own benefit. They will accept laws and rules, but often mayhem, chaos, resistance, and disorder precede the acceptance. And then there are those stalwarts who do what they want, when they want, to whom they want. To the rest of the country, that would seem strange. In New York, it's called being a New Yorker.

For decades, crime and New York City seemed synonymous, especially in Manhattan. Roving gangs, Murder Inc., drugs—over the years, they all played a role in the city's frightening notoriety. But those are the headline-making crimes. Living day to day in New York is often like avoiding potholes: you never know when you're going to trip over an idiotic law or ridiculous regulation that you must ignore or break, illegal though it might be.

Today, thanks to Disney and watchdog mayors, there is less crime but much more disorder in all the boroughs of New York. And as any New Yorker will tell you, rules are made to be broken. So is the law.

## Beyond the Law

In 2003, police arrested and charged a 54-year-old lawyer in connection with a bizarre kidnapping. The man, a long-time Tribeca resident, was well respected and known as a devoted Downtown Little League father.

Lawrence Omansky was charged with kidnapping his estranged real estate partner, binding him with duct tape, and keeping him in a tiny space beneath the floor of Omansky's apartment for 28 hours.

The victim, Lawrence Schlosser, a real estate investor, went to Omansky's home to tell him that he no longer wanted Omansky to manage a building they co-owned. A fight ensued, and according to Schlosser, Omansky punched him, threw him onto a bed, and held a knife to his throat while threatening to kill him.

Omansky bound and gagged Schlosser, and left him while he went out for two hours. When he returned, he had papers with him that he forced Schlosser to sign, turning over several pieces of real estate to him. Schlosser was restrained again with duct tape, and put through a trap door in the bathroom floor of Omansky's converted fire house home into the narrow space beneath.

Schlosser struggled to free himself, finally finding a piece of pipe he used to bang open the trapdoor and emerge hungry, thirsty, and filthy, but otherwise unharmed, 28 hours later.

Omansky surrendered to the police, but denied charges of first degree kidnapping and coercion and was released on bail. His lawyer claimed the case would be viewed merely as a business dispute. Ultimately, all charges were dropped—the prosecution did a little investigating into Schlosser himself and soon realized they might not be able to substantiate his story.

## Shameful History

On the night of February 28, 1741, a chain of events began at Broad and South William streets in Manhattan that became known as the "Great Negro Plot," one of the most tragic chapters in race relations in the city's history. On that cold evening, someone broke into the home of Robert Hogg, who lived at the corner of Broad and South William. Some time later, Hogg's stolen linens somehow found their way into the hands of John Hughson, the unscrupulous and shady owner of a tavern that catered to slaves.

Within the next few weeks, a series of mysterious fires occured. Determined to make a connection between the fires and the robbery, authorities arrested and questioned Hughson's young servant girl, Mary Burton. Offered money and threatened with eternal damnation of her soul, Mary told authorities of a plot to burn the city and kill all the white people, except her boss Hughson who would then be crowned "King of New York."

Naturally, the prospect of a slave revolt infuriated the white colonists who went on a rampage that ended with the execution of 31 African Americans, many of whom were burned at the stake. Another 154 were thrown in prison, and 71 were sent to the West Indies. Eventually, the truth came out that Mary was lying, but Hughson and his wife were executed for receiving stolen goods.

## Riker's Island

Riker's Island is 415 acres in the East River between Queens and the Bronx. It has 10 jails and 15,000 inmates, making it the world's largest penal colony. Schools, medical clinics, chapels, gyms, grocery stores, a barbershop, a power plant, a tailor, bus depot, and even a car wash reside here.

## Island Independence

Staten Island residents voted to secede from New York City in 1993, but such a move would require state approval, which they did not get.

## The Sushi Memo

A partner of a leading New York City's law firm set one of his paralegals a rather strange research task—to find the best sushi in New York City. The worker took the job seriously and interviewed lawyers and staff members at the firm, as well as searching on the Internet and critiquing restaurants. The paralegal produced a three-page report, with footnotes, including two attached menus. The report did the rounds of all the major legal companies in New York who believe it accurately shows the bizarre climate that many paralegals work in. Many young law employees are required to work on every small task that their boss demands of them, however trivial.

# Loony Laws That Still Exist

- Anyone swimming in a New York City pool must have mesh lining in their swimming trunks.

- In New York, it is legal to teach your pet parrot to speak, but if he squawks, you're breaking the law.

- It is illegal to shoot rabbits from the back end of a Third Avenue streetcar when it is moving.

- In New York, it is unlawful for any person to do anything against the law.

- Donkeys are not allowed to sleep in bathtubs in Brooklyn.

- All new buildings around Times Square are required by law to put up massive billboard-style advertisements.

- A person can be sent to jail if he opens his umbrella in the presence of a horse in New York City.

## Feeding Frenzy

Law-abiding Pedro Nazario fed the birds outside his Harlem home every day for years. On his 86th birthday, he learned that he was breaking the law. As he scattered crumbs, he was approached by a policeman and issued a summons in violation of health code 431-22 for feeding pigeons in public. It was considered a misdemeanor and Pedro risked a fine of up to $1,000.

## Quality of Life Crimes

A man in Queens was fined for sitting on a long-abandoned milk crate outside a hairdressing salon. The crime—against quality of life in New York. A first violation for this offense carries with it a fine of $300, and up to $600 for subsequent violations.

An Israeli tourist was also caught by a quality of life crime. He spent over a hundred dollars on New York souvenirs but was forced to hand over all the goods to pay for his fine. The police charged him with the crime of falling asleep on a subway train and allowing his head and arm to fall onto the next seat.

Another strange quality of life crime concerned a woman who was fined for putting her handbag on the adjoining seat in an almost empty train car.

## Demonstration of the Dispossessed

On March 6, 1930, during the Great Depression, police attacked 35,000 unemployed New Yorkers demonstrating for government aid.

## Mystery of Marie Roget

A boarding house on Nassau Street was home to Mary Cecilia Rogers, a lovely young woman who sold cigars and tobacco in the neighborhood. She disappeared on July 28, 1841, and her strangled body was found floating in the Hudson River. Her murder was never solved. Edgar Allan Poe, an admirer of Mary Cecilia and a frequent visitor to her tobacco shop, later based his story, *The Mystery of Marie Roget* on this case.

## Don't Bank On It

52 Wall Street was the first and long-time home of City Bank, now Citibank. America's first bank robbery took place here on Sunday, March 20, 1831, although the theft was not discovered until Monday morning when the bank opened. Over $200,000 in bank bills and two hundred Spanish doubloons were stolen. A man by the name of Edward Smith was caught within a week, and sentenced to five years in Sing Sing for his crime.

# A Fatal Love

The sensational stabbing murder of Dr. Harvey Burdell took place on January 30, 1857, at his Bond Street home. Emma Cunningham was the one-time lover of the well-known dentist, as well as a boarder. Upon his death, she quickly declared that she was his secret wife and thus entitled to his estate. Immediately suspicious of such a claim, the authorities arrested her, but since a murder weapon could never be found, she was acquitted for insufficient evidence. Cunningham was not willing to give up, however. She then pretended to be pregnant with his child, but this deception was exposed when the police caught her trying to buy a newborn baby.

## Environmentally Unfriendly

For years, a Bronx businessman diligently recycled his old newspapers—until he was fined for tying up his bundle the wrong way. He put them at the curb in cardboard boxes, with never a question from the garbage collectors or his neighbors. But a diligent policeman—perhaps the same one who took the Israeli's souvenirs as punishment for napping—fined the Bronx limousine company boss because he should have been tying up the papers with string and putting them in clear plastic bags on the sidewalk.

# Matrimonial Strife

New Yorkers cannot dissolve a marriage for irreconcilable differences—unless they both agree to it! That rarely happens, of course, since one party will usually say "no" to the other about something, or why else would there be a reason to end the marriage? If a partner says "no" to the divorce, the other has to prove that the disputee was at fault. There are four legal faults, and at least one has to be legally proven:

1) If one spouse has abandoned the other, meaning they have left their domicile for over a year.

2) If there hasn't been sex for a year.

3) If one spouse has treated the other with physical or mental cruelty. Pictures of bruises taken in the emergency room are considered good, but not foolproof evidence.

4) If one has committed adultery.


Proving fault keeps New York marriages lasting longer than they should while the lawyers get fat and happy. Divorce is easier and cheaper in New York if one spouse has been in prison for two or three years. It seems that committing a crime is the most legal route to divorce.

## Smoke 'Em Out

Smoking is banned in all New York bars, restaurants, bingo halls, and betting shops. Since the ban came into effect, there have been thousands of noise complaints, an increase of almost 200 percent from any previous year. The complaints are about smokers congregating outside bars at night.

## Smoking Stinks

Anti-smokers living above bars are furious because of fumes wafting through their windows. Some have taken the law into their own hands, dumping garbage and eggs on the smokers below. Wonder if dropping garbage on someone's head qualifies as a "quality of life" crime?

## Marlboro Munchies

Another restaurant has resorted to cooking with tobacco. The owner rolls his own cigars in the skin of green apples. Dishes include homemade gnocchi with Empire English special blend tobacco; filet mignon with Golden Virginia tobacco; and Tobacco Panna Cotta, a tobacco Grappa to finish the meal.

## Cycling Slip-Ups

The police in New York are required to fine cyclists for coasting along with their feet off the pedals and for not having bells on their bicycles.

## Wheels on Fire

A Brooklyn legal secretary discovered she was on the wrong side of the law when she received a parking ticket for parking in her designated spot outside her apartment. It seems the wheels slightly overlapped her parking line.

## Kosher Water

Restaurants and bakeries that operate under Orthodox Jewish Law use special filters to ensure water purity because of the discovery of tiny creatures called copepods in the tap water. Copepods are crustaceans which are barred from consumption under Jewish law.

## Too Much, Too Late

A New York appeals court ruled that Leon Caldwell was entitled to a $50,000 state worker-compensation death benefit on behalf of his son, Kenneth, who died at the age of 30 at the World Trade Center on September 11, 2001. Even though Leon had abandoned Kenneth shortly after his birth and only seen him twice since, the court said that Leon "met the legal definition of a parent." However, the court ordered Leon to pay Kenneth's mother $20,000 in back child support.

## A Helping Hand

A bar in Soho offers its patrons free pieces of Nicorette™ chewing gum.

## Parking Prohibitions

It is against the law in New York City for a vehicle to idle for more than three minutes while parking or standing, except if you are loading or unloading. Violation can cost anywhere from $220 for a first-time offense to $875 for a repeat crime.

## Doctor's Riot

On April 13, 1788, the Doctor's Riot broke out on the first site of New York Hospital on the West Side at Broadway and Thomas Street. Some boys had observed medical students in a doctor's anatomy class working on cadavers. Word got out and rumors of body snatching inflamed a crowd which set out for the hospital. The next day, the jail where the doctors and students had taken refuge was stormed by the self-proclaimed militia who killed five people. The following year a law was passed allowing only the corpses of executed murderers, arsonists, and burglars to be used for medical dissection.

## Scene of the Crime

A robber stole $10,000 from a New York City bank. He was arrested after being spotted at the same bank four days later—asking to open an account.

## Five Points

The most infamous slum in New York City was Five Points—a five-pointed star formed in the 1800s by the intersection of several streets downtown. By 1850, the

> The Irish population in the area was second in size only to Dublin.

Irish population in the area was second in size only to Dublin. Densely populated, it was home to 270 saloons and over 500 brothels.

New York: the only city where people make radio requests like: 'This is for Tina—I'm sorry I stabbed you.'

– Anonymous

## Mother Mandelbaum

The most successful fence for stolen property ever recorded in the annals of New York City crime, resided in a small frame house on Clinton Street. "Mother" Fredericka Mandelbaum started in 1862 and continued to ply her thriving business for the next 20 years. During that time, it is believed that she handled almost $10 million in stolen goods. "Mother" weighed over 250 pounds and was committed to giving others an education: she gave lessons in pickpocketing and burglary to eager students. When the police finally shut her down, she fled to Canada.

## Inflation Choke

In December 1935, Mayor LaGuardia of New York prohibited the sale and possession of artichokes at the Bronx Terminal Market to end the inflation of their price by organized crime.

## Third-Degree Burns

Thomas F. Byrnes was a detective and superintendent of police in Manhattan, and became widely known in the 1880s when he solved the robbery of $3 million from the Manhattan Bank. In 1883, he persuaded the state legislature to place all precinct detectives under the command of his headquarters. Until then, the primary activity of these detectives had been to collect payoffs for the precinct captains. Byrnes advanced to the rank of chief inspector in 1888 and became superintendent of the police force in 1892.

> A vicious and brutal man, Byrnes has been given the dubious credit of inventing the third-degree form of questioning.

A vicious and brutal man, Byrnes has been given the dubious credit of inventing the "third-degree" form of questioning. Byrnes amassed a fortune of $350,000 upon his retirement, some of which came from payoffs he had received from the underworld. Byrnes was blamed for not arresting Mother Mandelbaum earlier in her career, no doubt looking the other way in exchange for payoffs from the notorious fence herself.

## Den of Thieves

The worst tenement was called the Old Brewery. A large wooden structure, surrounded by alleys, it was built in 1792 and condemned as a brewery in 1837. Once the workers abandoned the building, the poorest of the local population moved in. One section was called the Den of Thieves. Another was Murderer's Alley. At night, cries for help could be heard coming from Murderer's Alley. At least one murder a day took place there; there were 5,000 recorded murders in a 15-year period. The police seldom entered the building, even though they knew crimes were being committed there and known felons lived there. If the police did go in, they would do so in armed groups of at least 40 or more. Any fewer and the police would be murdered. This was such a fiendish place that it was not uncommon for children born in the Old Brewery not to see daylight until they reached their teens.

## Trial by Media

A brothel at 41 Thomas Street was the scene of a grisly ax murder on April 10, 1836. Helen Jewell was a beautiful, charming, and highly literature woman who read poetry—she was also one of the city's best-known prostitutes. Her lover, Richard Robinson, a 19-year-old shop clerk, was the last person to see her alive and subsequently arrested. This was the time of the "penny press," the new mass-circulation daily newspapers who competed vigorously for readership and there was a lot coverage in these publications during this murder trial. Robinson was eventually acquitted by the jury, as well as the press who felt that he had done the community a service by killing this celebrated sinner.

## Sickles' Cell

In the 1860s, Philip Barton Key, the son of Francis Scott Key, creator of *The Star-Spangled Banner,* was shot and killed at a Fifth Avenue townhouse. The murderer was Daniel Sickles, a U.S. representative, who resented Key's attention to Sickles' wife. At his trial, Sickles was the first person in the United States acquitted on a plea of temporary insanity.

# More Loony Laws

- The penalty for jumping off a building is death.

- A person may not walk around on Sundays with an ice cream cone in his pocket.

- It is illegal to shake a dirty mop out of a window.

- It is against the law to throw a ball at someone's head.

- It is illegal to slurp soup.

- It is illegal to start any kind of public performance until after 1:05 P.M.

- It is illegal to carry an open can of spray paint.

- A man can't go outside while wearing a jacket and pants that don't match.

*New York City is the most exciting place in the world to live. There are so many ways to die there.*

— Comedian Denis Leary

## Pull the Rug Out From Under You

A young couple moved into a downtown loft and discovered that the previous owner had left an expensive and elegant antique Persian rug rolled up in a corner. Thrilled at their good fortune, they unrolled the rug—and discovered the remains of a corpse in it.

## Burial Ban

The oldest burial site in Manhattan is the First Sheareth Israel graveyard at 55 St. James Place. Burials at the site span from 1683 to 1825, until, in 1851, New York City legislation outlawed burial anywhere within Manhattan.

## Potter's Field

There are an average of 2,650 unclaimed burials each year in New York City's Potter's Field on Hart Island, located in Long Island Sound about 20 miles north of the city. It is New York City's cemetery, and was originally used as a concentration camp for Confederate POWs after the Civil War. The desolate 101-acre island was also an installation for seven years during the Cold War for the "Nike" guided, surface-to-air missiles.

## School's Out

Before 1935, children who had reached the age of 14 were legally allowed to drop out of school to work full time. After 1935, the age was raised to 16, which stands to this day.

## Laws of Length

It is a law in New York City that the length of any single vehicle, inclusive of loads and bumpers, should not be more than 40 feet. A sedan limousine is usually about 18 feet long, while a stretch limo, which is created by slicing a car in two and inserting a midsection, is about 22 feet. If the "stretched" part—measured from the rear edge of the original front door to the front edge of the original rear door—exceeds 100 inches or a little more than eight feet, the builder has to certify that the limo meets additional safety requirements before it can be driven.

# Still More Loony Laws

- In New York City, jaywalking is legal as long as it is not diagonal.

- It is also illegal to throw swill in the street.

- You cannot have a puppet show in your window.

- A permit is required to transport carbonated beverages.

- While riding in an elevator, one must talk to no one and keep his hands folded in front of him while facing the door.

- It is illegal to wear slippers after 10:00 P.M.

- Citizens may not greet each other by "putting one's thumb to the nose and wiggling the fingers."

- It is against the law to burn offal or bones, or grow ragweed in New York City.

## Water Retention

In 1991, due to drought conditions in New York, water-on-request became a rule in the City of New York. This meant that any restaurant who doled out water without being asked for it by the patron was subject to a fine of $100, that could jump to $500 for repeat offenders. That rule is still on the books despite New York's reservoirs being filled to capacity.

## Stonecutter's Riot

When construction began in 1834 on the first buildings of New York University, contractors used prisoners from Sing Sing Prison in upstate New York to cut the marble. The hiring of these inmates led to the Stonecutter's Riot, the first labor riot in New York City.

## Pete's Tavern

Pete's Tavern at 129 East 18th Street opened in 1864, and is the oldest continuously operating bar in New York City. Posing as a florist shop, it was a speakeasy during Prohibition and the thirsty customers would enter through a refrigerator in the back of the shop.

## Curb Crawling

An average of 110,000 people are arrested annually by the sanitation police for stealing newspapers and corrugated cardboard from curbs in the city.

## Rent by the Hour

A new trend in prostitution in New York City is for prostitutes to rent vans or limousines and ply their trade from the vehicle in a parking lot. The parking lot attendant receives a few dollars for the hourly rate in addition to a "tip" of a few dollars for looking the other way. This saves the cost of a hotel room, and for the customer, it eliminates the risk of vehicle impoundment if arrested for visiting a prostitute. If a call girl is arrested, the vehicle rental company has to pay the fine for the impounded van or car, usually not a problem for the company since it generates a lot of income from the arrangement. There used to be over 400 prostitutes walking down 11th Avenue between 23rd and 44th streets each evening—before the advent of "quality of life" crimes.

## Undercover Agents

There are 4,300 transit police in New York City, and 10–15 percent are undercover. No other city in the country has a full-time police decoy unit aside from New York City. About 155 arrests are made each year by undercover subway police pretending to be drunk and asleep.

## Death by Magic Marker

In 1984, Michael Stewart was beaten to death by members of the New York Police Department for the crime of writing with magic marker on a subway wall. All the cops were acquitted.

## Bare With Me

Transit police decided that women who ride the subway topless would not be arrested or ticketed. This conforms to a loony law still on the books that says women may go topless in public providing they are not doing it for business.

## Towed Away

Around 35,000 cars are towed annually for parking violations in New York City.

## Give Me Shelter

There are 75 police precincts in New York City, with approximately 38,400 police officers, including both the Housing Police force and the Transit Bureau. Thirty-seven policemen form a special team created specifically to persuade the homeless to move to shelters.

- It is illegal for a father to call his son a "faggot" or "queer" in an effort to curb "girlie behavior."

- You may only water your lawn if the hose is held in your hand.

- You cannot smoke within 100 feet of the entrance to a public building.

- It is illegal for a woman to be seen on the street wearing "body hugging clothing."

- It is against the law to leave a mannequin undressed in a shop window.

- Yet completely legal for the giant department store Macy's to sell used underwear.

- The maximum penalty for begging is 10 days in jail.

## Flirting With Danger

A fine of $25 can be levied for flirting. The law specifically prohibits men from turning around on any city street and looking "at a woman in that way." A second conviction for a crime of this magnitude calls for the violating male to be forced to wear a "pair of horse-blinders" wherever and whenever he goes outside for a stroll.

## Jury Judgment

New York is the only place that does not require jury sequestration in felony cases.

## Freedom From Poverty

In 1831, New York became the second state after Kentucky to outlaw imprisonment for poverty.

## Ellis Island

After the heyday of immigration, Ellis Island operated as a hospital for soldiers as well as a detention station for deportees and illegal aliens. When the island was abandoned in 1954, there was just one inmate—a sailor detained for the crime of overstaying his shore leave—who needed to be rehoused.

## Gang Warfare

An estimated 3,000 teenagers pledge allegiance to one of 125 gangs in New York City each year. This number does not include the 100 different tongs/gang organizations in Chinatown.

> The elderly couple's dog bit and deeply scarred the child's nose and cheek during her birthday party in NYC.

## Family at War

The parents of a four-year-old girl have filed a $1.2 million lawsuit against the girl's grandparents. The elderly couple's Akita dog bit and deeply scarred the child's nose and cheek during her birthday party in New York City. The grandparents are being sued by their own son who works as a lawyer, as does his wife.

## Strong Medicine

In 1916, one-third of the city's habitual drug users were supposedly addicted to heroin. The narcotic was originally touted as a cough suppressant and was manufactured by the Bayer company.

## Opium Opulence

In 1896, there was an estimated 25,000 opium or "hop" users in New York City. The heroin boom started in 1870 when two opium dens opened. Wealthier opium smokers at the turn of the century would bring their own gold, ivory, or silver paraphernalia to drug dens that had sprung up throughout Manhattan, particularly in Chinatown. People sometimes stayed in these opium dens for weeks on end, and in the fancier ones that catered to a more elite clientele, there was even entertainment by piano players.

## Flying High

At the turn of the 19th century, cocaine was cheap and readily available in drugstores throughout the city. Considered to be a "poor man's high," the drug was injected with a needle until snorting became fashionable.

In the Tenderloin section of the city at 40th Street and Seventh Avenue, the Lafayette Hotel featured a backroom with a potted tree called the Burny Tree (crystallized cocaine was called "burny"). The tree's branches were decorated with hundreds of lengths of black rubber tubing used for snorting cocaine.

## Pot for Purchase

Marijuana was also readily available in drugstores at the turn of the 19th century, but was not as popular as either opium or cocaine.

## Drug Traffic

Over 8,300 drug dealers move through the New York City criminal justice system annually.

## Nature Lovers

A wave of plant and tree thefts plagued 102nd to 110th streets near Riverside Drive in 1995.

## Cabbies in Court

New York City hosts a special court that hears about 400 complaints a day against taxi drivers. A cab driver, recently immigrated from Pakistan, found himself in this court because he had punched a passenger. Asked why, the driver said: "In my country, women aren't allowed to speak disrespectfully to a man." In another case, a professor from Columbia University took a cab driver to court because he had made a face at how small the tip was.

## Bee Keeping

The police and the fire departments are the official city agencies that deal with bees.

## Underwater Police

The New York Police Department has an official scuba squad of about 20 divers, and at least half are on duty at any given time. Half of the dead bodies found in New York City's waterways are found in April and May. The average number of bodies found in the rivers each year is 20, although 1984 was a particularly unpleasant one for the scuba squad: they found 92 bodies in various city rivers. The East River and the Harlem River are the most popular for dumping bodies.

## Day of Rest

A law passed in 1641 forbids drinking on Sunday during church hours. New Amsterdam residents violated the law so flagrantly that a more strident ordinance was passed in 1656 which prohibited playing tennis, dancing, any manual labor, sowing, mowing, fishing, hunting, gambling, card-playing, cricket, boating, building, frequenting taverns, having or attending parties, playing ninepin, and cart-riding. The citizens who ignored the law as well as those who flaunted it by providing liquor and other amusements were fined.

## Class Conflict

On average, 13 New York City teachers are assaulted each day, with at least five requiring medical attention.

## Lawless Lessons

The average number of weapons confiscated annually in New York City public high schools is around 8,000.

## Court by Candlelight

On September 1, 1907, New York City was the first in the country to conduct a session of night court.

## Lindbergh Ransom

In April 1932, at St Raymond's Cemetery in the Bronx, Bruno Hauptmann received the $50,000 ransom in gold certificates for the promised return of the kidnapped Lindbergh baby. The baby was never seen alive again and Hauptmann was subsequently charged with the child's murder, after the discovery of $13,000 of the ransom money in his garage and the recovery of a $20 gold certificate from his jacket pocket.

New York: Where everyone mutinies but no one deserts.

– Harry Hershfield, cartoonist and columnist

## Murder Inc.

Murder Incorporated was the nickname used for an organization of criminals based in the Brownsville section of Brooklyn in the 1930s. They carried out contract killings for a nationwide organized crime syndicate. Sicilians and Jews largely controlled the firm, and its ten leaders included notorious and powerful men such as Lucky Luciano and Albert Anastasia, who was popularly known as the "lord high executioner." Estimates of the number of murders committed by the organization range from 400 to a thousand. It disbanded in 1940 when several lower-level criminals were arrested and provided information to the district attorney of Manhattan. This led to the arrest, prosecution, and ultimately the execution of Louis "Lepke" Buchwalter, one of the ten leaders, as well as several other members.

### Accidental Death

The federal appeals court in New York ruled 2-1 that when a man died of "autoerotic asphyxiation" (translated: strangling oneself almost to the point of passing out as a way of enhancing pleasure during masturbation; in some cases, going too far and dying), it was deemed an "accident" rather than a self-inflicted injury. As a result, the man's mother was entitled to the death benefits under her son's life insurance policy, which she would not have received for a self-inflicted injury.

## A Law Unto Herself

In 2004, a New York City judge was criticized by the police for helping a convicted drug dealer escape out of a side door of her courtroom, so that he could avoid a detective poised to arrest him for a robbery that had occurred the month before. The judge said she was angry that the detective hadn't cleared the arrest with her in advance. The judge, Laura Blackburne, already had a reputation for an odd form of leniency and reading of the law. She released a man charged with attempting to kill a police officer, ruling that the would-be murderer had not received a speedy trial and so his rights had been violated. Blackburne was reassigned to the civil court after the scandal.

## A Case of Mistaken Identity

Police charged a 32-year-old New York City salesman with assault. That would not be unusual in itself; however, the nature of the assault turned out to be a bit different. According to police, the man's live-in girlfriend arrived home unexpectedly after he had just put in an order for a call girl to come over to the apartment. The man improvised a plan to intercept "Jasmine" in his building's lobby, have a quickie in the basement laundry room, then dash back upstairs before his girlfriend got suspicious.

When he saw a good-looking woman in the lobby, he assumed she was the prostitute. He nudged her into an elevator and began to paw and fondle her while waving around a $50 bill. The woman turned out to be an assistant district attorney from Brooklyn.

## Private Eyes

In 1845, George Relyea and two partners opened the first detective agency in the United States. At the time, New York was the only city in the country with a police force, but as their jurisdiction ended at the city limits, criminals who fled from the city were not usually pursued. Detective agencies began to spring up as the city's criminal activities increased. The public did not quite trust detectives who felt they were in cahoots with the criminals, especially with thieves. When the detectives retrieved stolen goods, no one ever quite believed all of the loot was returned to their rightful owners.

Another frowned-upon part of the detective agency work was looking into the backgrounds of potential suitors. A branch of the Pinkerton National Detective Agency was formed in the city in 1865 and reassured its customers by refusing to work for rewards and by seeking the arrest and prosecution of those it apprehended.

Pinkerton did not completely eradicate the more unsavory detective agencies, especially those who conducted espionage in the workplace—such as using "spotters" on streetcars to catch conductors who kept, or knocked down, the nickel fare. Detectives were also criticized for operating such organizations as the Association for the Suppression of Gambling and the Society for the Prevention of Crime where they would observe criminal activity and then report the customers to their employers.

Today, private detectives use similarly unscrupulous practices—landlords in New York City hire private eyes to determine whether rent-controlled apartments are, in fact, the tenant's primary residence, so the landlord can evict the tenant and put the apartment on the market for much more rent.

## Chief of Corruption

William S. "Big Bill" Devery was the Chief of Police in the late 19th century—but he wasn't a particularly law-abiding citizen! Devery worked as a bartender at a tavern in the Bowery, but he didn't believe this was his life's calling. He knew he could make much more money as a cop, so he paid a bribe to Tammany Hall and became a policeman in 1878. His rise up the ladder was swift: he was promoted to sergeant in 1884, captain in 1891, and then achieved a major coup by running the Eldridge Street Station in a well-known red-light district where graft was frequent and plentiful. Proud of being corrupt, Devery would have his aides approach saloon owners before an election, promising protection if they voted for the Tammany ticket. Then, in 1898, "Big Bill" was named Chief of Police and his riches accumulated even more. In 1901, the Tammany boss was defeated and Devery lost his position, but his wealth assured him a very comfortable retirement.

## Fighting Back

A woman in the Bronx came home to find a man who had broken into her apartment was still there. He ran past her and down five flights of stairs into the street. The woman decided she was not going to let the intruder get away with it, and immediately gave chase. When she reached the street, a construction worker pointed to a taxicab in which the robber was now sitting. Without thinking twice, the victim opened the cab door and yanked the man out of the car, causing his head to get knocked on the door. As the thief was being pulled out, he tried to hit the woman, but she ducked, knocking the man back down. She told him she didn't want to hurt him, but he wasn't going anywhere until the police arrived. They soon did, along with the paramedics as the man had suffered an asthma attack.

## Losing Your License

A man in Queens broke into a man's home using a card—however, the card he used was his own driver's license. Instead of sliding the card in and out to open the door, the thief inserted his license completely. It jammed in the door and refused to come out, so the robber left, furious. He then filed suit against the people of the house—the people he was planning to rob—for losing his license.

## Telltale Tip Line

New York City decided to help relieve its budget woes by creating the Snitch Tip Line. In an attempt to cut down on the number of fraudulent legal claims against the city, residents are asked to snitch on people they believe are trying such scams. More than $600 million is paid out annually, many to people filing false claims against New York City, but there is not enough time, manpower, or money to investigate all the cases. A claims fraud task force was created and the Snitch Tip Line will be an important source of information for them.

## Cold War

Two Bronx ice-cream vendors were charged with attempted murder for a pipe attack on two of their competitors. It seems that one husband and wife ice-cream selling team had been in constant dispute with the alleged attackers over routes for their competing ice-cream truck operations. One Saturday night, the wife was held down by the competition's wife while the competition's man beat her in the head with a lead pipe. When the victim's husband and their 15-year-old granddaughter tried to intervene, they were also attacked. The 64-year-old victim ended up in the hospital with skull fractures and internal bleeding. Her husband and granddaughter were not seriously injured.

## No Care at Day Care

The story of Matthew Perilli struck fear into the hearts of working parents all over New York. According to police reports, little Matthew was in his playpen in a busy day care center run by Heather Zlotshewer. She was downstairs talking to a health inspector after the city's health department had closed an unlicensed center she had been running. The official wanted to see the upstairs room, but Zlotshewer falsely explained that only her own child and his friends were playing there. However, reports suggested that eight babies and two three-year-olds were upstairs—too many for the care assistant to be legally looking after by herself.

When Zlotshewer checked on Matthew, she saw that the two three-year-olds had piled heavy toys on him, thinking it was a game. Matthew was not breathing, and she raced with him to a nearby hospital where he was pronounced dead. The case went to court and the death of Matthew Perilli at Devlin Daycare in

Forest Hills, Queens, was ruled a homicide. No charges have been brought against Zlotshewer, although an investigation took place which resulted in the firing of the Health Department's bureau chief who was responsible for the city's 9,400 day care centers.

## Dumb and Dumber

An Oklahoma car thief drove 1,750 miles to get arrested for trying to sell a stolen car on eBay. The man had 30 offers for his Corvette, and he clicked on a bid from undercover New York City detectives who knew the car was stolen. They agreed on a cash price, and the thief drove two days to New York City where he was met by the police officers in the garage of the Hilton Hotel.

## Automobile Audacity

Two New York men were pulled over for driving too slowly when the police discovered they were driving a car that had been reported stolen a month earlier in upstate New York. The two men were on their way to the Brooklyn courthouse, where prosecutors had agreed to a plea deal for them to have only three years in prison for their roles in a crack-cocaine ring. The deal was ended and they received much stiffer sentences with the stolen car charges added on.

# Down the Back of the Sofa

A couple from Texas were indicted in Manhattan federal court for narcotics conspiracy and possession with the intent to distribute 400 pounds of cocaine with a street value of $8 million. It seemed that the couple had used a truck and trailer to transport a sofa filled with cocaine from El Paso, Texas to Manhattan. The U-Haul trailer and truck had been abandoned on Manhattan's Upper East Side, and had several parking tickets. A man's name was handwritten on the truck's temporary Texas license plate. The New York Police Department notified U-Haul about the trailer, which was taken to a rental center in the Bronx. The sofa was left for sanitation pick-up, but when they heaved it into a city garbage truck, fine white powder filled the air as the truck's compactor crushed the sofa. The couch was traced back to the couple in El Paso, where they were arrested.

## Drive With Caution

A 40-year-old man who sped off after crashing into another car on Staten Island, got lost and decided to ask directions from two police officers getting into their patrol car. It turns out that the police were actually looking for him as they had received a phone call from the man whose car had been hit, giving them a description of the driver, as well as his license plate.

## Diplomatic Relations

The husband of a diplomat (a senior diplomat at the Bangladesh Mission to the United Nations) claimed he was stripped of almost $130,000 dollars at a New York City topless club. He filed suit, charging that the strip club ran up bogus charges on four of his credit cards. $130,000, it turns out, would pay for 6500 lap dances or buy 40 bottles of the most expensive champagne.

## Dangerous Dog

Staten Island was the scene of a *Man Bites Dog* headline turned reality. It all started when the police received a call that a man would not leave a woman's home. By the time officers arrived, the man had beat up his girlfriend, set two grass fires, and run. The fires were easily extinguished, and the police soon found the culprit hiding nearby, refusing to come out. A police dog was sent in to get him, and bit the suspect on the leg, as he had been trained to do with recalcitrant suspects. The man responded by lifting the dog off the ground and biting him on the head.

## Barking Mad

A New York City lawyer acted on behalf of a man who represented designers of home furnishings. The client was suing a couple for non-payment of fees incurred after marketing their products. During the depositions, the defendant gave sworn testimony that he had received letters from the attorney that he termed threatening, and called them "mad dog lawyer" letters. As the depositions continued, the lawyer in question began to bark like a dog and was fined $8,500 for misconduct and harassment of opponents. His client also found another attorney.

## Let Them Eat Cake

An inmate who claimed he was locked in his cell for taking an extra piece of cake in the mess hall sued—and was awarded $200 in damages.

## Idle Inmates

In the 1980s, New York's non-violent offenders were allowed to choose sidewalk sweeping or trash collecting instead of jail time. Of the first one hundred, 97 chose jail time.

## Briefcase Bungle

During World War I, Heinrich Albert was a German spy in the United States when he took a New York City subway, carrying a briefcase with plans to sabotage American factories. He left the briefcase on the train and American agents who had been following him, looking for the proof to make an arrest, found it.

## Undercover Civilian

A Staten Island man was arrested in an incident during which he pretended to be a cop. A 45-year-old man was driving near the beach in New Dorp when, for seemingly no reason, he hit the gas and tried to mow down two pedestrians. He then stopped the car, got out, and started to verbally abuse the two men, accusing them of being in his way. When they threatened to call the cops, the driver told them that he was one. He returned to his car and sped away. The two pedestrians not only got a good look at the guy but also enough digits on his license plate for the genuine police to pick up the driver and charge him.

## Mirthful Mugging

A 17-year-old wannabe crook in Brooklyn approached three men on a Crown Heights street, pulled a knife and demanded money. The men laughed and laughed, then they took away the knife and called the cops.

## Barber Bust

One Sunday morning, a 37-year-old man waiting at a bus stop in Brooklyn was approached by two men. Seemingly friendly, they chatted amiably until they jumped him, leaving the victim unhurt but taking his knapsack and running away. What they later found was the man's barber equipment.

## Pushed Too Far

A New York City sanitation worker took his job a bit too seriously. Outside a Washington Heights clothing store, the corner trash can was always filled to the brim with the store's trash. One afternoon, the worker had had it, and started screaming obscenities at the

> One afternoon, he had had it, and started screaming obscenities at the storefront window.

storefront window, yelling that they should stop putting the garbage in the garbage can. The manager stepped outside in an attempt to calm down the ranting sanitation worker who then grabbed a discarded plastic bucket—which had once been the shop's and was now in the trash can—and hurled it at the store's front window, shattering it. The sanitation worker returned to his depot, where he was promptly arrested and charged with criminal mischief. The store manager explained that they dispose of their trash properly in the dumpster out back, but that homeless people go through it, take stuff and throw out what they don't want in the city's trash can out front. He charged the sanitation worker with $100 to replace the broken window.

## Luckless Ladies

Two young women hailed a cab in Manhattan and provided an Upper East Side address as their destination. Upon their arrival, they didn't pay the fare, but instead announced that this was a robbery, and they had a gun so the driver better give them his cash. The cabbie did as he was told, but then the two women—instead of quickly disappearing down the street or into the subway—ran into the apartment building where one of them actually lived. The cabbie reported them to the police who found them in the apartment and arrested them.

## A Good Day's Shopping

Two female crooks visited an extremely upscale jewelry store on Madison Avenue in Manhattan. The crooks, looking as well-groomed and wealthy as most of the shop's clientele, were welcomed into the store by the security guard at around noon. The ladies, both young, said they wanted to buy a bracelet or a ring for their mother. As the saleswoman showed them a selection, they each took a gun out of their purses and ordered the entire staff into the bathroom. Calmly, with their guns pointed at the security guard, they ordered him to get the store's surveillance tape and also to gather all the jewelry from the display cases and safe. Part of their bounty included several watches priced between $3,800 and $4,900 and two rings valued at over $25,000 each. They gathered the jewelry into a bag and fled in a waiting car driven by a third female. On a busy lunchtime on Madison Avenue, no one thought twice about the pretty young girls driving off—with thousands of dollars of stolen merchandise. They still have not been caught.

## Caught in the Act

The Trump Park Avenue Hotel has a luxurious gym for its guests as well as Manhattan residents who can pay the steep membership fees. One late afternoon, a young woman emerged from the bathroom after her workout to discover another woman with her hand in the victim's locker, holding the victim's wallet. The caught thief did not apologize, explain, or confess. Instead, as the victim took back her wallet, the crook only said that she understood how she must be feeling, the same thing had happened to her recently. Incredulous, the victim promptly reported the attempted theft to the gym staff and the suspect was held until the police arrived and arrested her.

# If You Can't Stand the Heat

At a fancy restaurant on Third Avenue in the Upper East Side of Manhattan, the kitchen staff was relieved when the last diner had gone for the night. They were ready to clean up and do a little preparation for the next day. At 1:30 in the morning, however, the police received a 911 emergency call from the restaurant where they found a 16-year-old New York City boy who had been working in the kitchen. He was bleeding heavily from his arm, explaining that he had accidentally fallen on a knife. What the police discovered after some investigation was that a co-worker had become angry when they were playing a game with a knife and decided to convert the game piece into a weapon. The victim underwent surgery and his "game" partner was arrested for assault.

## Murder Most Stupid

The Ruth Snyder and Judd Gray murder, also known as the "Dumb-Bell Murder" is one of the most infamous in New York City crime annals. Their real crime, however, was being stupid.

Ruth Brown Snyder met corset salesman Henry Judd Gray while having lunch one afternoon in New York in 1925. Ruth was tall, blonde, and attractive. Judd Gray, two years older, was an instantly forgettable short man, with thick glasses.

Despite their differences, they began a sexually torrid affair. Ruth's husband, Albert, the art editor of a magazine, was never home during the day so Ruth and Judd had their trysts at Ruth's home when her nine-year-old daughter, Lorraine, was still in school.

Ruth Snyder decided that she wanted out of her marriage and began to work on Judd, saying that her husband mistreated her and had to be eliminated. Judd objected, but Ruth would not be denied. She pestered him so much that Gray began to drink prodigiously, with Prohibition liquor that he had to obtain illegally.

Finally, on a cold, raw day on March 19, 1927, Gray finally gave in to Ruth— the deed was to be done that night. The plan they concocted was for Gray to take a train from New York City to Syracuse, New York, and from there a bus to Long Island and the Snyder home. Gray hovered around the Snyder house, stopping under street lights to take swigs from his flask, as if hoping to be spotted and arrested before he could commit murder for his lover. Being as non-descript as he was and given the miserable weather, no one paid him any notice.

He entered the house through the back door, as he and Ruth had planned. The Snyder family was away at a party so Judd was to wait in a spare room where Ruth had left a window weight, rubber gloves, and chloroform. When the Snyder family returned around 2:00 a.m., Ruth opened the door to the spare bedroom a crack, whispering, "Are you in there, Bud, dear?" She soon returned wearing a slip, and she and Judd had sex with her husband asleep down the hall. Afterward, Gray took the window sash weight and Ruth guided him toward the master bedroom. Gray raised the sash weight and brought it down on Snyder's head, but it was a weak blow that merely glanced off his skull.

As cold and heartless as a seasoned killer, Ruth grabbed the weight from Judd and crashed it down on her husband's skull, ending his life. Judd and Ruth went downstairs for a drink before continuing with their plan, which was to fake a robbery by knocking over some chairs and loosely tying Ruth's hands and feet. Judd left and Ruth, who had been left conveniently near her daughter's bedroom, began banging on Lorraine's door. Ruth told Lorraine to get help, but instead of using the telephone, she ran to their next door neighbor who called the police.

Damon Runyon, the New York newspaper columnist, eventually wrote that Ruth and Judd were "inept idiots" and called the whole mess the "Dumb-bell Murder because it was so dumb."

The police arrived and from the beginning, they realized something smelled fishy. All of the items that Ruth claimed had been taken by the mysterious "burglar" were found by the police hidden in the house. The minute they began to question her, she confessed, blaming everything on Judd Gray. He was found a few hours later, back up in Syracuse in his hotel room which Ruth had supplied. He insisted he had never been in New York, but during a routine search of the room, the police found his train ticket stub in the garbage can of the hotel room. He broke down and confessed, blaming everything on Ruth Snyder.

By the time the case went to trial, the former lovers were vicious enemies. The case and trial captured media and public attention, much like certain infamous trials do today. Ruth and Judd had separate attorneys, each arguing their client's innocence. Ruth's case was that her husband drove her out of the house because he was still in love with a former sweetheart—a convenient explanation that could never be verified because both Albert and the woman in question were dead. In addition, Ruth's lawyer claimed that Gray had tempted her into murder by convincing Ruth to take out a $50,000 double indemnity insurance policy on her husband.

Ruth took the stand, playing the suffering wife as she had been well rehearsed to do. She testified that it was Gray who told her to take out the heavy insurance policy on Albert, and that Judd had even sent her poison to give to Albert. Judd Gray was in the courtroom throughout the proceedings, and when Ruth made the statement about the poison, he grew extremely agitated. Then it was his time to take the stand. His lawyer claimed that his client had been completely duped and dominated by Ruth Snyder; he had been a law-abiding citizen made mad by passion and lust. He insisted it had been Ruth who had taken out the insurance policy, and that it had been Ruth who dealt the deadly blow.

The jury was out a total of **98** minutes before returning with a verdict of guilty for each of them. Their sentence was death. Neither Judd nor Ruth could believe the jury had found them guilty. Judd Gray was executed on January 12, 1928, Ruth Snyder a few minutes later. This case became the basis for James M. Cain's famous, *Double Indemnity*.

## Money Muscle

Twenty ATM machines have been stolen in Manhattan. Since each one weighs 350 pounds—without money in them—police are looking for a gang of hefty thieves with trucks.

## Bringing Home the Bacon

A Queens bank teller was caught out when a client noticed that his deposit slips hadn't been properly validated. He brought this matter to the attention of the bank who called the police. They were able to work out which teller was supposed to have made the deposits, and tracked her to her home where they found $190,000 in cash—it took the police 10 hours to haul it out and then invoice it.

## Celebrity Crime

CNN news anchor in New York City, Jack Cafferty, discovered the hard way that celebrities are not exempt from the law. Cafferty pleaded guilty to leaving the scene of an accident after hitting a bicyclist in midtown. The bicyclist suffered minor injuries, and Cafferty was ordered to pay a $250 fine and perform 70 hours of community service.

## Park Avenue Attack

In October 1986, CBS anchor Dan Rather was beaten by an attacker on Park Avenue. Rather sought refuge in a nearby building lobby, but the attacker came after him, knocking Rather down and kicking him repeatedly in the kidneys and neck. The assault was particularly odd as the attacker kept shouting the phrase, "What's the frequency, Kenneth?" Rather had no idea what this referred to and the incident inspired lots of theories as to the identity of the attacker, as well as the REM song "What's the Frequency, Kenneth?" Years after this incident, the same attacker was arrested for fatally shooting an NBC technician outside the studio offices.

## Fashion Victim

A young man attempting to break into a clothing store in the Flatbush section of Brooklyn was squeezing himself between the metal bars of the rear window of the store when his sweater caught in the bars. In the process of trying to free himself, the thief slipped and the sweater tightened around his neck, choking him to death.

## Waste Not, Want Not

There once was a New York City art lover who decided to steal five antique silk prints enclosed in glass from an airline lounge at Kennedy Airport. The prints, owned by Alitalia Airlines, were valued at $5 million, and had been on display in the first class lounge, but were taken off the walls as the airline was in the process of moving to another terminal. The thief claimed he thought the airline was throwing them away, so he took them home to hang in his apartment. He might have gotten away with it, too, if, when he was grabbing for the paintings, he hadn't accidentally dropped his dental appointment card, complete with his name and phone number.

## Red-Light Rockefeller

The area where Rockefeller Center is located, between 48th and 51st streets, and Fifth and Sixth avenues, was previously a notorious red-light district owned by Columbia University. Campaigners tried to clean up the area and it was originally designated as the new location for the Metropolitan Opera, before being sold to the Rockefellers.

# A Step Too Far

The Taxi and Limousine Commission of New York City sometimes takes its job too seriously. Legendary television newsman and intrepid *60 Minutes* reporter, Mike Wallace found himself handcuffed and shoved into a TLC car during a confrontation that was bizarre from beginning to end. Wallace had called ahead to a favorite neighborhood restaurant on the Upper East Side to pick up his dinner at around 8 P.M. While he was inside, waiting for his order and chatting with the owner, two TLC officers outside started questioning Wallace's limousine driver who was double-parked in a black Lincoln Town Car.

Wallace, alerted to the situation, came out, wanting to know what was going on. One of the TLC officers accused him of giving him lip, although Wallace had merely asked what was happening. He stepped into his limo for a moment, then got back out, but the cop ordered him back in the car. Eyewitnesses verified all of this. Before he knew what was happening, one officer grabbed him, pushing him up against the car, and twisting his arms behind his back, yelling, "I'm going to arrest you!" Wallace fought back only by saying, "I'm 86 years old! I'm a reporter, not a criminal." The two TLC officers refused to stop, and they hauled Mike Wallace off to the 19th Precinct stationhouse, where he was hit with a disorderly conduct summons and released.

## Bouncing Checks

A man from Queens tried to deposit two forged checks into his personal bank account. The teller felt something wasn't right about the checks and asked him to wait a moment. She went to the back and called the police. The checks were a bit larger than what she usually saw. One was for five billion dollars and the other for six billion. The man was arrested.

## Slacker

A man from Brooklyn went shopping, picked up a pair of slacks, and tried them on in the dressing room. He liked them so much he kept them on and walked out of the store without paying for them. He was quickly apprehended, given that he had left his old pants in the changing room—with his wallet and ID.

## Who Wants to be a Millionaire?

A woman tried to open a charge account in a New York City department store by flashing a piece of paper currency in the amount of $1 million. There is no such bill. She had made her own by pasting 0's on a one dollar bill and then running it through a color copier. While she was waiting for approval on her credit application, the police arrived and arrested her.

## Father Christmas

A mother took her son to a store in Brooklyn to see Santa Claus. When the little boy sat down on Santa's lap, he looked at him, then turned to his mother and said, "Daddy is Santa." Sure enough, the mall Santa was her ex-husband, who was wanted by the police for failure to pay child support. Santa, who began to scream at his ex-wife, was subsequently fired for frightening the other children.

# PART III:
# Urban Myths

*This metropolis has all the symptoms of a mind gone berserk.*

– Isaac Bashevis Singer, *The Cafeteria*, 1986

*It couldn't have happened anywhere but in little old New York.*

– O. Henry, *A Little Local Color*, 1910

By its very definition, a myth or legend need not be proven. Authorship is not nearly as critical as credibility. In a place like New York City, an environment rich in strange people, weird events, and apocryphal tales, the urban myth has become a veritable art form, a new kind of literary endeavor that takes its place alongside open mike poetry as a way to mitigate the dullness of ordinary existence. But, in New York, ordinary existence is an oxymoron, whether myth or fact. And for New Yorkers, the true measure of qualifying for entry in the annals of urban mythology is whether, indeed, it could have happened—but only in New York.

Late night talk show hosts, alternative newspapers, web sites, bars, restaurants, offices—no place and no one in New York City is immune from "Did you hear the one about…?" The remarkable quality about the urban myth as it exists in New York is the ardent desire of people to buy into it and believe. For all their arrogant sophistication and cultivated skepticism, New Yorkers are almost childlike in their willingness to accept what any country rube would know to be not only false but patently ridiculous. And even when an urban myth can be proven to be an invention of a clever and active imagination, somehow, in New York City, the legend lasts—if it is interesting enough, weird enough, edgy enough. If it is New York enough. Here are some examples:

## Unholy Graves

At one point in time, Jesuit priests who taught at Fordham University in the Bronx were buried on the school's ground. When some of the land belonging to the university was sold to the New York Botanical Garden, the headstones were removed, but the bodies were not—so the legend is that Jesuit priests remain in unmarked graves at the New York Botanical Garden.

## Hoffa in the End Zone

Jimmy Hoffa, the Teamster leader, is reputed to be buried under an end zone at Giants Stadium in the Meadowlands. Gangster Donald Frankos turned state's evidence and joined the witness protection program, testifying that the Teamsters' boss was murdered in Michigan and his body kept for five months inside an oil drum. Legend has it that, some time later, Hoffa was eventually brought to New York, and then buried in the Meadowlands Sports Complex in New Jersey during its final stages of construction.

## Movie Extra

In the movie, *Three Men and a Baby*, there is the ghostly figure of a boy sitting at an apartment window with a shotgun in his grip. According to legend, a nine-year-old boy committed suicide with a shotgun in the very same Manhattan apartment just a few years earlier.

## The Money Train

One of the most persistent of urban myths is the Money Train, a subway train that supposedly picks up cash from all the token booths in the city and funnels the money to an undisclosed location. On any given Money Train ride, millions of dollars are channeled through the city's subway system. A movie called *The Money Train* was even made about it. There is even talk of a Money Room for the Metropolitan Transit Authority, the world's busiest private currency processing enterprise and the only one of its kind to operate 24 hours a day.

## Subway Shock

In another popular legend, a drunk man on a subway platform relieved himself on the tracks and was electrocuted when his urine hit the live rail.

## Don't Lose Your Head

Another often told tale is how a construction trench collapsed in New York City one winter, burying a worker up to his neck. Emergency crews were summoned, but before they could arrive, a co-worker manning a backhoe tried to dig him out, and accidentally decapitated him.

## The Penny Drops

Legend has it that coins dropped from the top of the Empire State Building can kill pedestrians or embed themselves in the pavement. In truth the aerodynamics of the skyscraper create a hefty updraft that actually blows any tossed coins back against the building, where they usually land on window ledges on the 86th floor.

## Dog Foo Yung

"Chinatown restaurants regularly serve up cat and dog meat." No one is really willing to find out the truth behind this myth.

# A Croc Of...

• At one point in time, some New York tourists who visited alligator-friendly Florida decided to bring back a batch of tiny baby alligators as a memento of their trip. Growing bored with their new pets, the New Yorkers flushed them down the toilet and into the sewer system, where they continued to grow, breed, and create an underground colony. Deprived of sunlight, the alligators become blind and albino. Feeding this rumor, in 1935, the *New York Times* reported an incident in which some children living in Harlem fished such an alligator out of a manhole.

• Police apparently took an emergency call from some people who had seen a four-foot-long alligator strolling through a park in Queens. Police and city park rangers captured the animal with a noose and took it to a reptile specialist at the Bronx Zoo.

• A two-foot-long baby spectacled caiman, a member of the crocodile family, was supposedly captured in Central Park by an alligator wrestler from Florida and his wife. City park officials determined that the reptile was probably someone's pet and had been dumped in the Harlem Meer after it got too big, as when a pet alligator outgrew its owner's bathtub and was dumped in Kissena Lake in Queens.

## Oyster Bar Echo

By standing at opposite ends of the hallway in front of Grand Central Terminal's famed Oyster Bar, people can whisper to each other in perfect clarity.

## Rat Delight

A hapless rat fell into a fast-food fryer, and apparently ended up being called Crunchy Chicken Delight when it was served at dinner.

## Suicide or Murder?

A man who jumped off the top of the Empire State Building to commit suicide was said to catch a stray bullet on the way down. The story goes on to say, police charged the man who fired the shot, during a squabble on the ground floor, with murder.

## Hot-Dog Hokum

Supposedly, a busy hot-dog vendor in New York City can make more than $80,000 a year. Then again, the gastroenterologist treating food poisoning cases from that same vendor can make more than $300,000 a year.

### Property Tycoons

Columbia University is purportedly the second largest landowner in New York City, after the Catholic Church.

### Executive Etiquette

Some say young Wall Street executives are being sent to take a course on how to use a napkin and the correct way to hold a knife and fork.

### Tusk Unearthed

When the Harlem ship canal was being dug, a workman is said to have discovered the tusk of a prehistoric mastodon, 12 feet beneath what is now Broadway and 14th Street.

### Stuyvesant's Spirit

Years after his death, the ghost of the last Dutch governor of New York, Peter Stuyvesant, was seen roaming through his former mansion at Third Avenue and 10th Street, and in the chapel of St. Mark's Church, where his crypt is. Legend says his appearance was in protest against the paving of the church's yard to make Second Avenue.

*No matter how many times I visit this great city I'm always struck by the same thing—a yellow taxi cab.*

— Scott Adams, American cartoonist

## Commuter Crush

Another cautionary urban legend tells of a careless commuter who fell between the station platform and the oncoming train. As the engine screeched to a halt, the victim was spun around violently and wedged between the cars and the platform. Horribly squashed, the pressure of the train kept the victim in place against the station floor. Then, when the train began to move again, his internal organs ruptured from the pressure, and he died.

## Costly Cake

It is said that a patron at one of the Waldorf-Astoria's restaurants loved the chef's fabulous red velvet cake, and sent word to him through the waiter that she would like a copy of the recipe. The waiter returned with the recipe on a printed card, and a bill for $500—for the recipe alone. Consulting with a lawyer proved useless: he told her that since she asked for the recipe, she had to pay the bill. To get even, she then distributed the recipe to everyone she knew for free.

## Travel Sickness

There are many urban myths about people dying while using the city's public transport system. In 1999, a 37-year-old man supposely died on a New York subway during the morning rush, but was not discovered until hours later. He was found in a sitting position, his head tilted slightly down, eyes closed like a typical rider taking a catnap before his stop.

In 2000, it was claimed that a 61-year-old New York City bus passenger died on the bus and was found only when the driver went to shake him awake at the last stop.

## Deadly Current

It has been rumored that a woman arrived home in Queens to find her husband being electrocuted in the kitchen. He was shaking frantically, with a wire running from his waist toward the electric kettle. Intending to jolt him away from the deadly current, she retrieved a plank of wood that was by the back door and whacked him with it, breaking his arm in two places. Unfortunately, it turned out that all he had been doing was dancing along to the music on his CD Walkman.

# Lions On the Loose

On November 9, 1874, the front page of the *New York Herald* warned that the animals had escaped from their cages in the New York Zoo and were rampaging through the city. A lion had been seen inside a church and a rhinoceros had fallen into a sewer. The police and National Guard were trying to do battle with the beasts, but already 27 people had died and 200 were injured. The *Herald* reported that the editor of the *New York Times* had run out of his home waving two pistols in the air and berating the police for not doing more. It turned out that the entire story was a fabrication by the *Herald* as a way to draw attention to dangerous conditions at the zoo.

## Even Death in New York is Legendary

There is a story set in the mid-1990s about a young man who leapt off a Manhattan apartment building but was caught in a suicide net erected on the eighth floor to discourage jumpers. He died, but it wasn't the jump that killed him. An autopsy revealed that the cause of death was a shotgun blast to the head.

Given that he would have survived the jump by landing in the net, his death was ruled a homicide and a murder investigation by the New York Police Department was begun.

Interestingly enough, at the time of the jump, the New York Police Department received a telephone call from a woman in the same building. She lived on the 15th floor and reported hearing a gunshot from the apartment next to hers.

The responding officers to this call dispatched to the building found an old man and an old woman squabbling in their apartment. The old man was holding a 12-gauge shotgun. The argument seemed to be about who had loaded the gun since part of their "loving" relationship was when they were arguing, the old man would take the unloaded gun, point it at his wife, and pull the trigger. This time the gun had been loaded. The shot missed his wife, went through the 15th floor window, then blew away the head of the jumper as he was making his descent from the roof of the building.

The old couple swore that they never kept the gun loaded—it was a joke, nothing more. Further questioning revealed, however, that the only other person who had been in the apartment recently had been their son, an hour earlier. No, they didn't know where he had gone.

Meanwhile, in the murder investigation, the detectives learned that the jumper, Roland Opus (also sometimes reported as Ronald Opus), had been having serious financial troubles. His parents were quite wealthy, but they had cut him off because he wasn't making anything of his life. Further investigation revealed that the jumper's parents lived on the 15th floor of the very same building from which he had jumped. Everything began to come together, especially since the timing of the report of the shotgun going off and the headless jumper matched.

The jumper, Opus, had been in his parents' apartment on the 15th floor—the same old couple who liked to play with shotguns. Despondent over his financial problems and knowing of his parents' peculiar idea of fun, he loaded the weapon with some bullets that he had brought with him. Opus figured that one of these days his parents would go at it again. His father would threaten his mother with the shotgun, and pull the trigger. This time the gun would be loaded so his mother would be dead, his father arrested, and then the entire family fortune would be his.

But even the thought of considerable wealth was not enough to turn the tide of despair for poor Opus. Plus it also meant killing his mother and ruining his father, and while he had never been particularly fond of either, they didn't really deserve such miserable ends. So Opus decided to end his sorry existence.

So at the exact same moment Roland flung himself from the building, his parents were in the middle of one of their typical arguments. And in typical fashion, the old man pointed the gun at his wife and pulled the trigger. Now loaded, the bullet missed his wife but got his son, killing him instantly. Ultimately, Roland Opus' death was ruled death by misadventure, not murder, since, for all practical purposes, he had killed himself.

## Glove Giveaway

A subway commuter saw a businessman leave the train without a pair of gloves that were on the seat next to him. The commuter rushed to catch the man as the train door closed, tossing the gloves after him. As the story goes, when the train pulled away from the station, a homeless man who was sharing the same row of seats with the businessman demanded to know why the Good Samaritan threw his gloves out of the subway car.

## Thanksgiving Begging

Brooklynites claim a custom called Thanksgiving begging as a tradition they followed, rather than Halloween trick-or-treating. Instead, children would dress up as either Indians or ragamuffins, and on Thanksgiving morning go around to their neighbors asking, "Anything for Thanksgiving?" The tradition began in the early 1900s and came from a European custom of begging on holidays to give to those less fortunate.

This died out as Halloween trick-or-treating became more popular, although the Ragamuffin Parade in Bay Ridge is still held on the last Saturday of September or the first Saturday of October, when thousands of children dress up in costumes, many of them as ragamuffins.

# That Broadway Melody...

Broadway and the theater are ripe for legends. In the 1890s, even up to his death in 1931, the name of producer/impresario David Belasco was synonymous with the Great White Way. At the Belasco Theater on West 44th Street, he sat in his own special box during a production, only to rush backstage afterward to give his own critique of the performance. According to eyewitness reports, Belasco always dressed in a black suit and a white collar, priest-like. His apartment was upstairs in the theater where he liked to entertain beautiful actresses.

Shortly after Belasco died on May 14, 1931, people began to hear strange noises in the theater on 44th Street, especially on opening nights. There were reports of seeing the ghost of Belasco sitting in his special box, scowling if he didn't like the performance, as he would do when he had been alive.

The last "official" sighting was in the 1970s when the revue, *Oh! Calcutta!* was performed there. Since this was an all-nude show, those who claimed his ghost still prowled the theater determined he didn't appreciate the modern vulgarity of the play.

Things supposedly were quiet until around 1993 when a caretaker at the theater heard the rattling of the elevator chains to Belasco's apartment—where no one had lived since Belasco died.

## X-Rated ID

A woman who modeled in an X-rated magazine supposedly had trouble cashing a check at a New York City bank because she wasn't carrying a driver's license or any other form of identification. She was, however, carrying the magazine in which she appeared nude. So she handed the magazine over to the bank teller, hitched her sweater up to her chin while arranging herself in the same pose as she appeared in the magazine. Her check was cashed.

## Tank-Powered Police

There has long been a rumor that the New York City Police Department's arsenal includes two armored tanks. They are supposed to be 50,000-pound armored personnel carriers from the Korean War era, stripped of their weapons. Their purpose, if there is one, is to rescue officers or civilians pinned down by gunfire or to transport officers through areas threatened by gunfire.

Called ERVs, or emergency rescue vehicles, they have apparently been available but rarely used for more than 20 years. They reach a top speed of 35 miles an hour and can carry 10 people. Given a tank's lack of quick mobility, one has to question their effectiveness, especially in a city known for its traffic problems.

## Pepper Games

In Yankee Stadium, Pepper Games are prohibited. These are pregame warm-ups that involves a guy, a bat, and four or five teammates who stand around 15 feet away, pitching him balls. Each player takes a turn throwing balls to the batter who then hits a grounder to another player. The idea is to hit the ball in a different spot each time, controlling the bat when faced with pitches from the extreme left to the far right. What this has to do with pepper is the stuff legends are made of: speculation has it that it may have come from the expression, "to pepper the ball down the line."

## Poison Gown

In New York, there is the tale of a lovely but very poor young girl who was invited to a formal dance. She had nothing suitable to wear, but then a friend suggested she rent a costume for the evening. The girl liked the idea and decided to go to a pawnshop near her apartment. For a reasonable sum, she was able

At the dance, she was having a Cinderella fairytale kind of evening when she began to feel oddly faint and nauseated.

to rent a beautiful white satin evening gown with all the accessories. At the dance, she was having a Cinderella fairytale kind of evening when she began to feel oddly faint and nauseated. She fought against the growing discomfort as long as possible, but eventually she had to leave, barely making it into a cab and back to her apartment.

Once home, she collapsed on her bed, where her lifeless body was found the next morning. The unusual circumstances of her death led the coroner to order an autopsy.

It was discovered that the girl had been poisoned by embalming fluid which had entered her pores when she became overheated from dancing. The district attorney traced the dress back to the pawnshop where the pawnbroker reluctantly admitted that the dress had been sold to him by an undertaker's assistant. The assistant had taken it from the body of a dead girl just before her casket had been nailed shut.

## Burnside Avenue

There is a claim that the Bronx thoroughfare called Burnside Avenue is named after General Ambrose Burnside, a Civil War officer. His side whiskers were known as "burnsides" and then "sideburns," which they are still called.

# A Fishy Tale

In 2003, a fish heading for slaughter in a New York fish market apparently shouted warnings about the end of the world before it was killed. Zalmen Rosen, a Hasidic Jew, says coworker Luis Nivelo, a Christian, was about to kill a carp to be made into gefilte fish in New York's New Square Fish Market when the carp begin to shout in Hebrew about people needing to account for themselves since the end was coming soon. Mr. Nivelo was shocked, but Mr. Rosen didn't believe him. Nivelo dragged Rosen to the back of the market. The fish spoke again, identifying himself as the soul of a local Hasidic man who had died the previous year. The fish instructed Rosen to pray, but Rosen was in such a state of panic that he tried to kill the fish. Instead, he injured himself and ended up in the hospital. The fish was eventually killed by Nivelo and sold.

## Dividing Up Manhattan

The gullibility of New Yorkers is an age-old tradition, it seems. In 1823, a retired butcher named De Voe and a wealthy contractor named Lozier were at New York City's Center Market trying to get people to save themselves: Manhattan Island was sinking, they told the crowd. As America's most populous city, the combined weight of all the people, buildings, and infrastructure made Manhattan too bottom-heavy, and the island was beginning to sink into the harbor.

Even the skeptics in the crowd began to believe them when they claimed that New York's mayor Stephen Allen had hired them to find a solution to fend off the impending disaster. They were to oversee a massive effort to saw Manhattan in half, tow the lower half out into the harbor, turn it around, then reattach it. That way, the most heavily populated section of the island would be in the middle, thus producing a more balanced island. Incredible as it sounded, New Yorkers believed this story. After all, they had witnessed the successful development of the Erie Canal, so no engineering feat seemed impossible. Not only that, the city had recently been ravaged by an economic depression and a yellow fever epidemic, so the prospect of work was welcome.

> Lozier and De Voe signed up hundreds of eager workmen, craftsmen, and suppliers needed to saw the island in half.

Lozier and De Voe signed up hundreds of eager workmen, craftsmen, and suppliers needed to saw the island in half. It was determined that it would take 20 men per saw, provided they could demonstrate the ability to hold their breath while sawing underwater. Then they would need to row the dissected half of the island out past Governor's and Ellis Islands at an estimate of 100 men per oar, pivot the land, row it back in, and reattach it.

Carpenters and joiners were needed to fashion twenty 100-foot-long saws with three-foot teeth and two dozen 250-foot-long oars. Then blacksmiths and ironworkers were hired to make cast iron oarlocks and huge anchors. Contractors had to build housing for the workmen. Farmers and butchers had to supply thousands of cattle, pigs, and chickens to feed the massive crews.

On the day work was to begin, the workers arrived at the site and waited for Lozier and De Voe to show up. They waited in vain. Finally, a group was sent back to Center Market to find out what was going on. There they received the message that the two men had left New York owing to health problems.

To this day, there is little documentation that this episode in New York City history took place. It has taken on the dimensions of urban legend, which means it doesn't matter if it actually happened, New Yorkers continue to believe it did.

## Ghost Town

New York City ghost stories abound, and few dare to claim they are the stuff of myth and legend. One story is the haunting of the Empire State Building by a young woman in 1940s dress, who roams the halls, waiting for the young man who promised to meet her at the top of the building during V-J Day. The movie

*An Affair to Remember* helped to promote this tale. Then there's the ghost at the White Horse Tavern in Greenwich Village, supposedly inhabited by the famed patron who drank himself to death there, Dylan Thomas. Greenwich Village seems particularly ripe for hauntings. Chumley's, the Bedford Street speakeasy has over the years apparently played host to Henrietta, a long-dead bar mistress who occasionally comes in for her customary Manhattan. And the Ear Inn, on Spring Street in the Village, is home to Mickey's ghost, a sailor who was hit by a car in front of the bar.

Uptown, the ghost of Eliza Jumel—who purportedly murdered her husband Stephen in order to marry Aaron Burr—

> Many of the workers claimed they often saw a beautiful young woman wandering aimlessly and confused through the gutted theater.

roams the historic Morris-Jumel Mansion on 160th Street. And no one should forget Olive Thomas, a ravishing Ziegfeld Follies girl who died in Paris of syphilis in the 1920s. Not only might Olive's ghost be on the prowl, but it seems to travel as well—from Paris back to New York City.

When the New Amsterdam Theater on West 42nd Street, home to the Ziegfeld Follies, was renovated to house *The Lion King*, many of the workers claimed they often saw a beautiful young woman wandering aimlessly and confused through the gutted theater. She held a blue glass and was always dressed in a Follies costume with a sash that bore the name Olive. One time, a worker standing in the lobby heard a voice call out: "How are you doing, handsome?" However, when he turned around, there was no one there.

## Unwilling Donor

A group of Wall Street tycoons in the making decided to head over to the Waldorf-Astoria's famed Bull & Bear pub for an after-work drink. The bar, with its rightly earned reputation as a great pick-up place, worked its magic with one of the financial analysts who met a beautiful young woman staying at the hotel during her New York City visit. By the end of their second round of drinks, she was taking him upstairs to her room. At some point in the evening, he blacked out.

When the broker finally awoke, he found himself naked and half-submerged in a bathtub filled with ice. He climbed out of the bathtub, and groggily looked in the mirror. On his chest was lettering which he deciphered from the backward scrawl in the mirror. In lipstick on his chest were the words: "Call 911 or you will die." He couldn't believe it, but then he became aware of a pulling sensation in his back, and felt gingerly around. He turned sideways toward the mirror to see two sets of crude stitches on either side of his lower back. He realized that his kidneys had been stolen for sale on the black market—another victim of this popular urban myth.

## AIDS Mary

There is also the tale of AIDS Mary, an extremely attractive New York City woman who picked up men in bars, had sex with them, and then left them with a lipstick-written message on the bathroom mirror: "Welcome to the World of AIDS."

## Blindfolded Bike Ride

One day in 1945 it is said a man named Kuda Bux climbed onto his bicycle and pedaled into New York City traffic. He rode through busy Times Square where he finally stopped. There is nothing unusual about this, of course, except for the rumor that Bux was totally blindfolded.

## The Power of Touch

In 1963, Russian medical researchers were rumored to be fascinated by the case of Rosa Kuleshova. In several rigidly controlled experiments during which she was blindfolded, Kuleshova was able to read newsprint and sheet music with her fingertips and elbow. Dr. Richard P. Youtz, a psychologist at Columbia University in New York City performed several experiments of his own. He concluded that there were certain people whose skin was abnormally sensitive and could read sightlessly by picking up the amount of heat absorbed by different colors. As black print absorbs more heat and is warmer than the white page which reflects heat, some sightless people should be able to "see" with fingertips or elbows.

# The Case of the Creepy Church

On Grymes Hill in Staten Island, one of New York City's five boroughs, sits St. Augustinian Academy, once a boys' high school that closed in the 1960s. It later became a retreat that was shut in 1985, and today is supposedly abandoned.

To reach the monastery, one drives up a winding road through a quaint Staten Island neighborhood and there, on a secluded hill surrounded by trees, is a huge building. As the story goes, the front door remains wide open and inside there are long staircases. Going up the main staircase, one sees walls covered with graffiti and satanic signs. The building is roofless. And on the grounds, in the back, is a fountain shaped like a cross. There are three floors with around 30 rooms on each floor, and the basement goes down at least 10 floors underground. Bloody animals wrapped in cloth hang from the ceilings of several rooms. One level underground is a room with a giant stone in the middle, and there are wooden doors, marked as if they were locked from the outside and someone tried to claw his way out. The sounds of feet walking and people talking have been heard by intrepid visitors.

The urban myth surrounding the St. Augustinian Academy says that about 60 years ago, monks lived there in solitude and silence. There was, however, one monk who found the peace and quiet too much. He went berserk, going on a killing spree that ended with the massacre of all the other monks. The monks slept in sublevels that went underground 30 floors. But there was also one final, secret sublevel. The mad monk dragged the dead bodies of his brothers down to that secret sublevel and mutilated each of the bodies.

## Sleepy Store

Apparently a dead woman in a chair went unnoticed for four hours in a West Side Barnes & Noble bookstore. Patrons thought she was napping, which is not an unusual occurrence at the bookstore. Since a group of mystery novelists had been visiting the store that particular day, the event seemed particularly apt.

## Dead-End Job

Managers at a New York City publishing company were perplexed by the fact that no one noticed that one of their employees had been sitting at his desk for five days. Always the first to arrive each morning and the last to leave, seeing him at his desk all the time, nose buried in manuscripts, was not unusual. A proofreader at the company for 30 years, he had a heart attack on a Monday in the open-plan office he shared with 23 other workers. But it was an office cleaner on Saturday who realized something was wrong when she asked why he was working on the weekend and he never responded. As this urban legend shows, proofreading can be a dead-end job!

## Tammany Hall

The full name of the infamous Tammany Hall political machine was the Society of St. Tammany or Columbian Order of New York City. There was no St. Tammany, but there was Tamanend, a legendary Delaware Tribe chief known for his wisdom and devotion to freedom. In New York City about 1788, a "fraternity of patriots" formed a protest against the aristocracy and established Tammany Societies, elevating Tamanend to the stature of a saint as a way to thumb their noses at royalist organizations in America. So what became synonymous with political corruption began as a social organization.

## Port Ivory

Port Ivory on Staten Island was thought to have taken its name from herds of roaming elephants. Actually the name comes from Proctor & Gamble which built a huge 77-acre factory in 1907 on Staten Island. The area took the name of the company's most popular product: Ivory soap.

## Jewish Utopia

In 1905, the Utopia Land Company announced plans to build a new, cooperative town for Jews from the Lower East Side of Manhattan. The community was planned for 50 acres in north-central Queens, between what is now 164th Street and Fresh Meadow Lane, from the Long Island Expressway to Jewel Avenue. The north-south streets of Utopia were even to be given Lower East Side names like Division Street and Hester Street. But before lots could be staked out for the "perfect" neighborhood, funds ran dry and the land was sold, giving rise only to the Utopia Parkway, hardly ideal for anyone with a car.

## Owl's Head Park

Owl's Head Park in Bay Ridge, Brooklyn is so-called for one of two reasons, depending on which story one prefers. The first is that the area's shoreline once followed the contours of an owl's head, a fact impossible to prove by today's geography. The second purports that the 27-acre park was originally part of the estate of Henry C. Murphy, a wealthy Brooklyn editor and politician who framed the entrance to his estate with a pair of stone owls.

## Sheepshead Bay

Theories also abound about the name "Sheepshead Bay." One is that the area was shaped like the head of sheep before it was dredged and reshaped with landfill. More likely is that the primary residents of the bay waters were sheepshead, a greenish-yellow, black-striped relative of the bass, that once flourished in the coastal waters around New York before pollution took its toll.

## Bay Ridge

More than a century ago, the area now known as Bay Ridge was called Yellow Hook, a reference to the soil's makeup of yellow sand and clay. But when yellow fever swept through the area in the mid-1800s, the name Yellow Hook took on unpleasant connotations. The story goes that rich local landowners met to come up with another name, and one—a florist—suggested Bay Ridge to reflect the geographical formation of the land.

## The Source of Spring Street

Spring Street in Greenwich Village was supposedly named for a spring that was tapped by Aaron Burr's Manhattan Water Company in the late 18th century. However, legend has it that in 1800, the body of a young woman was found floating in a well on the corner of Broadway and Spring Street, minus her shoes, hat, and shawl. Her fiancé was arrested and charged with her murder, but then acquitted. There are still rumors of sightings of a gray-haired apparition wearing mossy garments.

## St. Paul's Pulpit

The carved pulpit at St. Paul's Chapel on Broadway at Fulton Street, topped by a crown and an array of feathers, is said to be the only surviving symbol of British rule in New York. St. Paul's Chapel is the oldest surviving church in Manhattan.

## Wolfe's Pond Park

Staten Island is considered the most haunted part of New York City—perhaps because of its remoteness from the other overcrowded boroughs. In Prince's Bay, one can enter Wolfe's Pond Park from the train station and follow the path down to a small, 20-foot cliff with a pond at the bottom. This is where, in the 1970s, two teenagers accidentally drove a car off the cliff into the water. The teenagers' bodies were not found for two weeks. People have experienced cold sensations at that spot and visions of a phantom car rolling and overturning in the pond.

> People have experienced cold sensations at that spot and visions of a phantom car.

## Tomb of the Unknown Visitor

Photos taken at the Vanderbilt Tomb in Staten Island's Moravian Cemetery have strange results. Either additional, unknown persons appear in the pictures when developed, or just the tomb appears with no image of the live people standing before it.

## In the Closet

Another Staten Island site, Kreischer Mansion, is tied to a tale of a young girl who got pushed into and locked in a closet. To this day, people report hearing mysterious banging noises, doors slamming on their own, and apparitions in the mirrors at the mansion.

## Richmond Apparitions

Richmond Town has a number of historical houses to visit, all between 100 and 300 years old, and all known to have spirits in them. The left-hand window of one particular house on a side street often hosts the apparition of a little boy—two young boys died in the upper level of the house. And in the small graveyard next to the old courthouse, a young broken-hearted girl has been known to wander around at night looking for her lost love.

## Fort Phantom

Fort Wadsworth in Staten Island has been the site of numerous ghost sightings. There have been tales of a mysterious soldier who walks through walls and moves cars around. One woman reported having a flashback to the time of the Civil War and seeing hurt and dying soldiers lying on the ground.

## Radio Reports

The College of Staten Island's radio station reports equipment running on its own and lights going on and off, with no electrical or human source.

## Redcoats Arisen

The Conference House at the foot of Hylan Boulevard in Staten Island is apparently haunted by Redcoats. When walking through it, you may feel someone tap your shoulder, or hear the faint sound of singing.

## Gunshot Ghoul

There is an abandoned building called Old Brier House on Staten Island. At 2 A.M. every morning, her family would hear gunshots coming from the basement, but when they would investigate, there was no one there— although the little girl who once lived there saw an apparition of a woman in a wedding gown.

## Creepy Canard

The ghostly face of a man who committed suicide in the 1890s regularly appears at a second-floor window of the old Canard Mansion on Staten Island.

## Freaky Factory

Disembodied footsteps and screams have been heard from within the abandoned cement factory on Staten Island. There have also been reports of a loud growl, voices, and on one occasion, the entire building shaking violently. Rumors also circulate about furniture moving around inside the factory—without anyone touching it. An eyewitness stated that he was in a room on the second floor, when a chair moved from the corner to the center of the room.

## Shadowy Specters

The Baron Hirsch Cemetery on Staten Island apparently hosts spirits dating back to the early 1800s. People who live in the neighborhood report shadowy figures seen around homes near the cemetery.

## Buttermilk Channel

The Buttermilk Channel runs between Red Hook, Brooklyn, and Governor's Island. According to legend, in the 17th century, the channel was so narrow and shallow that only cattle and flat-bottomed boats could get across. These boats were known as buttermilk boats for their regular trips to carry the preferred beverage of the Dutch from the dairies of Long Island via Governor's Island to New Amsterdam.

## Ant Eater

An intern doing his toxicology rotation at a Brooklyn hospital apparently fielded a call from an extremely upset woman who had caught her young daughter eating ants. The doctor explained that as ants were not harmful, there was no need to bring the girl into the emergency room. The mother calmed down and casually mentioned that she had also given her daughter some ant poison in order to kill the ants. The doctor urged her to bring her daughter into the hospital immediately.

## Toilet Trouble

It has been said that a Staten Island woman found a huge cockroach in her living room. She stepped on it, gingerly picked it up, and tossed it into the toilet. But the creature had only been wounded and continued to wriggle around in the toilet bowl, until a full can of insecticide was sprayed on it, killing it instantly. When her husband came home, he went to the toilet and lit a cigarette. He threw the butt into the toilet bowl, and the still present insecticide fumes ignited, seriously burning his more sensitive areas. When the paramedics arrived, they laughed so hard when they heard the story that they dropped the man's stretcher down the stairs, breaking his pelvis and several ribs.

# The Constellations

There is a debate that the constellations on the ceiling of Grand Central Terminal are actually arranged incorrectly. Legend has it that a commuter, a month after the terminal's opening, noticed that the stars were twisted around. Experts have said that the stars are reversed, going north to south, although there is a sign at the station saying: "Said to be backward, it's actually as seen from a point of view from outside our solar system." Astronomers claim that even from this view, the layout is wrong.

Original plans for the terminal, which opened at midnight on February 2, 1913, called for a skylight to be built in the suspended ceiling to provide natural light for commuters. The skylight idea was abandoned and designers worked feverishly to come up with alternative. An architect thought of the stars and hired a French artist to design the constellations and the lights to represent a night sky, while the paint would be sky blue to represent daytime. The starscape was drawn by a Columbia University astronomy professor.

The professor blamed the incorrect constellation arrangement on the painter, an Australian, who placed the diagram at his feet while painting instead of looking through the paper sketch. The stars were repainted in 1944; again incorrectly.

## Place for the Homeless

There are claims that 5,000 homeless people live beneath the streets of New York City, mostly in subway and railroad tunnels underneath Grand Central Station and Penn Station. Supposedly whole communities have sprung up there, with mayors, laundry facilities, electricity, and even an exercise room. The communities have teachers, a nurse or two, and "runners" who go to the surface to scavenge for food and supplies. Most of the mole people, as they are known, go for a week or more without seeing the light of day.

## Black Jack

Black Jack was one of the most popular chewing gums of all time. Manufactured by the American Chicle Company, the gum first appeared in New York City in 1870 when Thomas Adams manufactured it, calling it "Adams New York Gum No. 1." It was made from chicle, a form of sapodilla tree sap chewed in the Yucatan and Guatemala.

Legend has it that Adams tried unsuccessfully to use the chicle to manufacture rubber for carriage tires, but it was far more popular as a chewing gum, quickly replacing the chewable paraffin

*Legend has it that Adams tried unsuccessfully to use the chicle to manufacture rubber for carriage tires.*

wax people had been chomping on. Licorice flavoring was eventually added to create Black Jack. Although manufacture of the licorice-flavored gum gave way to other flavors, every now and then the gum reappears as a nostalgia item.

## Baseball Roots

The precise date and place of origin of baseball are subjects of heated debate between Manhattanites and Brooklynites. In 1846, a set of rules defining the "New York game" was issued by a committee of members of the New York Knickerbocker Club, an organization of wealthy men. Supposedly, these rules described a diamond-shaped infield with bases separated by 90 feet, a pitcher standing in the center of the diamond at a distance from the home plate of 45 feet, and other similar rules. During the next 15 years, 60 baseball clubs played in and around New York City.

As the city was so instrumental in the early development of the game, New York also claims to be the birthplace of several baseball traditions. It is said that New York fans were the first to eat hot dogs at a ballpark, introduced in 1900 at the Polo Grounds by Harry M. Stevens. Local fans were also apparently the first to hear the 1908 song, *Take Me Out to the Ball Game*.

## Trolley Dodgers

The name of the Brooklyn Dodgers baseball team, formed in 1883, is supposed to come from Brooklyn residents' skill at evading the streetcars of the trolley system.

## Bull's Head

A neighborhood in Staten Island known as Bull's Head is apparently named for the sign of a local tavern, which was adorned with a ferocious bull with large eyes and short horns. A church was later built on this spot, and its adjoining graveyard contains the body of Ichabod Crane, made famous by his friend, Washington Irving, in the story *The Legend of Sleepy Hollow*.

## Bottom's Up

New York City mythology claims a number of important alcoholic inventions: the Bloody Mary was first served at the King Cole Bar in the St. Regis Hotel by a Parisian bartender; the Manhattan was created at the Manhattan Club in 1874 to honor the election of Governor Samuel J. Tilden; the Bronx, consisting of gin, sweet vermouth, and orange juice, was developed at the Waldorf Hotel in 1906; the Christy girl—peach brandy, gin, and grenadine—started at the Sherry-Netherland Hotel; the Gibson, named for the illustrator Charles Dana Gibson, began its life at the Players Club; sangria first came to light at the Spanish Pavilion during the World's Fair of 1964–1965; and the kamikaze, a drink made with lemon juice, lime juice, cointreau, and vodka was introduced in 1972 at an elegant New York City French restaurant, Les Pyrénées.

## Let's Do Lunch

New York legend also claims the invention of a number of important edible items: the hero sandwich, Jewish champagne, alka seltzer, the Reuben sandwich, Yoo-Hoo (the chocolate drink), and the English muffin. New York City also has a love affair with sweets. Common knowledge—or accepted mythology—has New York City as the birthplace of the Tootsie Roll, named by its inventor for his daughter, and Chunky, named by its inventor for his granddaughter. The German immigrant Henry Heide is said to have sold more than 350 brands of candy from his shop in New York City, including Jujubes, Jujyfruits Red Hot Dollars, Chocolate Sponge, Mexican Hats, Parlay bars, and Turkish Taffy.

The ice-cream sandwich and soft ice cream known as frozen custard were also supposedly introduced in the city. And for the more health-conscious, yogurt became popular in the United States after two gentlemen named Daniel Carasso and Juan Metzger began producing it under the name Dannon in a small Bronx factory.

## Tin Pan Alley

Legend has it that the name Tin Pan Alley, the area where popular composers and music publishers were concentrated from the 1890s to the 1950s, came from the tinny sound of the pianos played by the songsters.

## Sewage Soaking

It was claimed that a bank officer flushed the toilet in the executive washroom and was blasted with a geyser of 200 gallons of raw sewage. He sued the Queens company where he worked, as well as the construction firm that neglected to inform anyone that they had shut off another sewer line, creating the added pressure that led to the disgusting explosion.

## A Clean Bill of Death

Nurses from a Staten Island hospital were supposedly baffled to find a dead patient in the same bed of a certain ward every Monday morning. No cause was apparent for the deaths—extensive checks on the heating and air conditioning systems and a search for a source of bacterial infection failed to reveal any answers. After further investigation, it turned out that on Monday mornings, one particular cleaner would enter the ward, remove the plug that powered the patient's life support system, and plug her floor polisher into the now vacant socket. When she finished, she would plug the life support machine back in and leave, unaware that not only was the patient dead, but that she had inadvertently killed him. The whirring of the floor polisher effectively drowned out any feeble calls for help from the dying patient. There were no legal repercussions, but an electrician was hired to install an extra socket.

> The whirring of the floor polisher effectively drowned out any feeble calls for help.

## Shock Tactics

There is a rumor that at least two fault lines run across upper Manhattan—one along 125th Street and another near Dyckman Street in Inwood. The last big earthquake in New York City was on August 10, 1884, measuring the equivalent of 5.5 on the Richter scale. The "experts" claim that the city is long overdue for a massive quake. Although some structures like the Chrysler Building and the Empire State Building were constructed to withstand that kind of shock, other fabrications, like brownstones, were erected before the age of modern construction techniques and could crumble. Worryingly, New York City has no building regulations to prevent earthquake damage, if there ever was one…

## Civic Virtue in Queens

Civic Virtue, a 57-ton marble statue, was made in 1914 by a Brooklyn-born sculptor to reside outside City Hall in Manhattan. The statue depicts a young man with sword raised over his shoulder, stomping on two defeated women at his feet who stand for vice and corruption. The statue is now in Queens—how it got there remains part of legend. One story says that the Queens Borough president in the 1940s wanted it there and paid to have it moved. Another story is that Mayor Fiorello H. La Guardia hated it so much that he banished it to Queens.

## Political Commentary: New York Style

An unknown "donor" to the Metropolitan Museum of Art is not exactly being thanked by their curators. One morning, they discovered a cartoon-like painting of President George W. Bush, set against a background of shredded dollar bills, hanging near an exit. A label next to the painting explained it was made with acrylic, legal tender, and "the artist's semen."

According to newspaper reports, anti-terrorist police units in New York have determined that the supposed semen paintings are not a biological hazard. This story could definitely be true; then again, it could also perhaps be another New York urban tale.

## Rude Reception

The story goes that during a swanky reception at the Plaza Hotel, a groom rose to address the assembled guests, instructing everyone to look under their seat. Taped under each chair was a photograph—taken by a private detective hired by the groom—of his best man and the bride-to-be in bed together. The groom announced that the marriage would be annulled the next day.

## Beauty at Any Cost

Another urban myth concerns a young fiancée who decided she'd look better in her white dress if she had a light tan. A week before her wedding, she went to a tanning salon. The staff warned her that for safety reasons, she should tan for only 30 minutes a day. But after the young woman had done her session, she decided she wasn't brown enough and went to another tanning salon the very same day. The staff there also told her she should tan for no more than 30 minutes a day, but she still wasn't satisfied and so went to a third tanning salon, and then a fourth. She did this for the next four days. Even though she was getting a little bit red, she felt she was going to look terrific in her white dress. Sadly, there was supposedly no wedding for this young woman. The day before the event, she was found dead—her internal organs had burned up from the tanning beds.

## Monkey Business

A grocery store in Brooklyn was supposedly the site of an unusual skirmish between man and beast. A monkey bit a toddler who was out shopping with his grandparents. The monkey's owner was a disabled man, confined to a wheelchair, who uses the creature to help him open doors and pick things up. The owner claimed the boy had been pulling the monkey's fur, causing the monkey to bite the child on the arm. The boy was treated at a local hospital and released, with no charges were filed. Although it is illegal to keep monkeys as pets in New York City, permits are given for those who help the disabled.

### Welcome to the Family

A couple allegedly rented an apartment in an "Italian Mafia" area of New York. When the pair came home one evening, they discovered that their apartment has been ransacked. After describing the event to one of their "wiseguy" neighbors, they were told to not call the cops until the neighbor made "a coupla phone calls." Some hours later, the couple answered their door to find some local people standing there with all of their possessions—courtesy of "the family."

## Bucket Beating

A bricklayer, working on a three-story tall chimney at a Queens home, set up a pulley system so his assistant could easily hoist up bricks to where he needed them. As they worked, his fellow builder complained about how difficult it would be to get the last bricks up to the flat roof of the building. At that moment, some new material was delivered and was placed on the roof by a fork lift. The bricklayer asked the driver of the fork lift if he wouldn't mind loading the rest of the bricks up there as well. Realizing he would not need his assistant any longer to help move the bricks, he sent him home.

When the bricklayer completed his work for the day, there were some bricks left over, but the fork lift driver had already left. Trying to figure out how to get the extra bricks down by himself, he decided to use the pulley he had set up earlier to lower them down.

Going back down to the ground, he raised a large metal bucket up to the roof level using the rope and pulley. He tied the rope onto a railing and climbed back up to the roof where he loaded the leftover bricks into the metal bucket. On the ground, knowing how heavy the bricks would be, he wrapped the rope around his hand a couple of time for leverage and then untied the end of the rope with his free hand.

The bricks were heavier than he realized. He was immediately and with alarming speed launched upward. On the way up, he met the bucket of bricks coming down with equal velocity. Something had to give. First it was the bricklayer's face as he collided with the bucket and broke his nose, then his shoulder which was dislocated. The bricklayer reached the pulley just before the bucket hit the ground, which broke a few of his fingers as they were pulled into the levering device. When the bucket hit the ground, its bottom fell out and the bricks spilled onto the ground. But the bricklayer's woes were not over.

As the light metal bucket raced back up, the bricklayer was hit in the groin when one of his legs stepped into the empty bucket. He then fell out of the bucket and landed right on top of the pile of bricks, breaking both feet. He collapsed in pain, but was grateful to be alive. He let go of the rope and began to cry out for help.

However, once he let go of the rope, the bucket had nowhere to go but back down—hitting him on the head and fracturing his skull. This urban myth provides a cautionary tale for any hard-working builder!

# PART IV
# Oddballs & Weirdos

Every person on the streets of New York is a type. The city is one big theater where everyone is on display.

— Jerry Rubin, social activist

They can be cranky, bewildered, giddy, frustrated, and sometimes moved to violence. In short, they [New Yorkers] are afflicted with the New York City Getaway Fever.

— Lucinda Franks, *New York Times* journalist

Perhaps nowhere else in the universe is being considered an oddball or weirdo as high a compliment as it is in New York City. From Staten Island to Brooklyn, in the Bronx and Queens, but especially in Manhattan, the ordinary is totally unacceptable. This is a city that embraces what it pokes fun at. The cold heart of the city beats hardest for those who dare to be different. That is why it is impossible, really, to label the "typical" New Yorker. Oh, sure, they can be surly, rude, cold. Talk too fast or walk too fast. But a true New Yorker is anything but typical. Whether it is with clothes, make up, and hairstyle; fusion of foods that have no business being together; ideas so far out of the box that they are peculiar enough to actually work; letters to the editor and call-ins to the radio stations—in all these ways and more, New Yorkers have proven themselves the quintessential urban oddity. Conformity is a cardinal sin to a New Yorker, yet it is one committed over and over again in the interest of being weird and strange and ahead of the pack. For every trend that begins in Los Angeles, New Yorkers will add a certain urban edge and claim it as their own. Soon, a uniform exists, worn by those in the know. But New Yorkers don't consider that conformity; it's being hip. And that is the difference between being weird in New York and anywhere else in the world. Everywhere else, odd is odd. In New York City, a little bit of crazy is a little bit of all right.

Then again, maybe everywhere else odd is odd, and in New York, what's strange is really, truly, no mistaking it—absolutely nuts!

## Crushing Greed

A man hit by a car in New York City got up uninjured, but lay back down in front of the car when a bystander told him to pretend he was hurt so he could collect insurance money. He did as he was told, and the car then rolled forward, crushing him to death.

## Smile for the Camera

A car thief was all smiles while he took pictures of himself with the camera he found in the car he was stealing in New York—but he forgot to take the camera with him when he finally ditched the car. When the victim got her car back and took the film in for developing, she didn't recognize a few of the photos—like those of the car thief. The pictures were extremely helpful to the police.

## Snowball Steal

As New Yorkers frolicked in the fresh snow after a winter blizzard, one enterprising young man set up a street-corner kiosk to sell snowballs for $1 each. He sold six, created a new inventory, then sold four more before calling it a day.

## Breath of Fresh Air

The going rate for breath consultants in New York City is $125 an hour. This gets the buyer a breath analysis using a gas sensor and a computerized gum thermometer. The sensor detects sulphur compounds, a by-product of bacteria in the mouth. You then get a breath make over.

## Test of Stamina

Author-athlete Sri Chinmoy sponsored an endurance race for runners in New York City in the late 1990s. The race was won by Istvan Sipos of Hungary, who finished the 3,100 mile course in 47 days, running from 6 a.m. to midnight. Four other runners competed on the concrete grounds of a Queens school, circling the facility about 115 times a day. The only prizes were a trophy and a photo album.

## Load of Garbage

A freelance photographer filed a $50 million lawsuit against the Waste Management Company for injuries, including brain damage, sustained while he was trying to take photographs at Ground Zero in New York in December 2001. The photographer had sneaked atop one of the company's garbage trucks to get a better shot when the driver pulled away, causing the photographer to fall which was, according to the suit the photographer filed, "a failure to respect his rights as a pedestrian."

## Lethal Dose

At Columbia University, American student Yao Cheng contaminated her dorm with the highly radioactive substance, phosphorus-32, in an attempt to force officials into letting her change courses. She stole the lethal isotope from the science department, and tried to reason that if she had to move dorms due to the contamination, they may as well let her transfer from biology to business studies.

# Historic Precedents for Being Peculiar

Edward Hyde, Third Earl of Clarendon, also known by the courtesy title of Lord Cornbury, was Governor of New York and New Jersey from 1701–1708. He was also America's first transvestite governor.

Known as a moral profligate, Cornbury was sunk in corruption, despised on both sides of the Atlantic, and considered the worst governor Britain ever imposed on an American colony. Characterized as a degenerate and pervert, he spent half his time dressed in women's clothes. He once expounded floridly in public about the "shell-like quality" of his wife's ears, inviting all the men present to feel for themselves. When dressed in his female garb, he liked to lurk behind trees and pounce on his unsuspecting victims. He was arrested once on Broadway by a patrolling watchman who mistook him for a prostitute. The colonists were not bothered by their governor's cross-dressing. What they did mind was that Cornbury would borrow money from just about anyone, and never pay it back. And who could say no to the governor?

A portrait of Lord Cornbury dressed in women's clothes hangs today in the New York Historical Society building. And the actor Cary Elwes can, if he so chooses, claim Lord Cornbury as an ancestor.

## Gun Slinger

Samuel Colt who invented "the gun that won the West" was a faculty member of New York University in the 1830s.

## Band-Aid

Robert Johnson, a Brooklyn pharmacist, invented the Band-Aid.

## Subway Slam

A 23-year-old man was hit by a subway car at New York City's 34th Street station when he leaned over the tracks to see the oncoming train, not realizing it was coming from the other direction.

## Libel Lunacy

A woman in New York City was on the run from the law on charges that she had destroyed property at her employer's home, while she worked there as a nanny. She was reading an article in the *New York Post* detailing what she had allegedly done, and she got very upset. So upset that she stopped a police officer in the street, showed him the article, and asked if he thought she should sue for slander. The police officer didn't know what legal action she should take, but he knew what he had to do. He arrested her on the spot and took her into custody.

## Two Men in A Boat

In 1896, two men, George Harpo and Frank Samuelson, set out from Battery Park and crossed the Atlantic Ocean in a rowboat.

## From Fighter to Writer

William Barclay Masterson, aka Bat Masterson, did what many transplanted New Yorkers do: he reinvented himself. After hanging up his guns in 1902, he became a sportswriter for the *New York Morning Telegraph*.

## Bottom of the Class

A New York City high school chemistry teacher reports daily to a do-nothing job, earning $77,000 a year. This is the result of his having been ordered out of the classroom for a variety of complaints and administrative findings. In fact, this man has spent about three-fourths of his time in the last 15 years in such jobs since New York City teachers are unionized and have highly generous job protections. For not teaching, this man has cost the school system about $600,000 in salary. Among the complaints against him are racist remarks to students (the teacher is African-American), insubordination, incompetence, improper grading, and sexual harassment. The teacher repeatedly has blamed bad administrators as the cause of all his problems. But he's not really complaining when he cashes his pay check.

*The overcrowding in the streetcars has impelled men to adopt the rule of hanging on to a seat when they get it. Occasionally I have seen a man give his place to a lady, but the act betrayed that he was from the provinces.*

— Mark Twain, New York City resident

## Cosmetic Crazes

One of the fastest growing surgeries is keeping New York City cosmetic surgeons busy—and that is nipple enlargement. According to one New York nipple surgeon, people do it to have the teasing look of an erect nipple all the time. Many men who do it are nipple fetishists who want their nipples to be super-sized. This is done with injections of collagen or cartilage taken from the patient's ear. There is also, of course, nipple reduction surgery, requested mainly by women who are self-conscious about looking too aroused in cold weather.

## Journalistic Integrity

A *Wall Street Journal* reporter wrote a story about how the *Boston Globe* was having trouble with columnists that made things up. He noted in his story in the *Journal* that the *Globe*'s corporate spokesperson had no comment on the matter, a fact which the *Journal* reporter later admitted he made up. He was subsequently fired.

*Each man reads his own meaning into New York.*

– Meyer Berger, New York Times columnist

## Mean Green

Henrietta "Hetty" Green was heiress to a $6 million fortune. In the late 18th and early 19th centuries, she became such a successful moneylender and shrewd investor in real estate, corporate bonds, and well-secured loans that she had a bank balance of $31,400,000 just in one account. But she lived in a seedy apartment in Brooklyn and did not allow any heating to be used, even in winter. She never bothered to wash and ate only a tin of dry oatmeal, which she would heat on the radiators at the bank. Her son had to have a leg amputated because of her delay in finding a free medical clinic. When she died in 1916, she left an estate valued at over $95 million.

## Tightrope Walking

Frenchman Phillippe Petit walked a tightrope between the rooftops of the World Trade Center towers in 1974. Thousands of people watched as 24-year-old Petit made eight crossings between the still unfinished towers, a quarter of a mile above the ground. The stunt took six years of planning.

## Toilet Paper Invention

Joseph C. Gayetty of New York City invented toilet paper in 1857. It was sold in packages of 500 flat sheets for the price of 50 cents a package. It was called therapeutic paper and was made of unbleached, pearl-colored, pure manila hemp paper and contained an abundance of aloe, a curative addition. Gayetty's name was watermarked on each sheet. It was marketed as "Gayetty's Medicated Paper—a perfectly pure article for the toilet and for the prevention of piles."

## Pet and Play

A New York mixer that encourages singles to meet through their dogs is helping lesbian, bisexual, gay, and transgender folks. The group is called Leashes & Lovers, and invites the lesbian, gay, bisexual, and transgender community to come out to their "poop and cruise" event with their dogs.

## Wigstock

Wigstock was begun in Tompkins Square Park in Manhattan in 1984, and is the largest drag festival in the country. It lasts all day and is totally free.

## Famous Hobo

Author Jack London once lived as a hobo in City Hall Park.

# Mayor Madness

The guy who inspired *Seinfeld*'s Cosmo Kramer character decided to run for mayor of New York in 2001. Kenny Kramer was a candidate of the Libertarian party, and believed that if a wrestler can become governor of Minnesota, what was to stop him from being elected mayor? Until this point in his life, Kramer's sole claim to celebrity was living next door to Larry David, *Seinfeld*'s co-creator, in Manhattan's Hell's Kitchen. Kramer is 58 years old, a Bronx native, who has held a variety of jobs including selling glow-in-the-dark disco jewelry, doing voice-overs for X-rated CD-ROMS, and the occasional gig as a standup comic. Given the fame that Michael Richards achieved as Cosmo Kramer on the show, Kenny Kramer has trademarked his name, and now has books, T-shirts, and even a reality bus tour through *Seinfeld*'s New York.

"If elected," Kramer said, "the first thing I plan to do is put my feet up on the desk, light up a cigar, and laugh my ass off."

In New York City politics, credentials are often the least important factor in getting elected.

## A Crying Shame

A 33-year-old woman was ordered to be held without bail on charges of second-degree murder. The criminal complaint alleged that at a midtown Manhattan homeless shelter, the woman held her son with his face down in the pillow until he stopped breathing. The mother didn't report the death, then claimed he had died a natural death. Eventually, she admitted she had to kill him—it was the only way to stop his constant crying.

## Tribal Tribute

At night during the summer of 1979, artist John Fekner painted the message, "Wheels over Indian Trails" in tribute to the 13 Indian tribes that once lived on Long Island. He painted this on the outside of the overpass of the Pulaski Bridge at the approach to the Queens-Midtown Tunnel. Two friends held on to the artist while he leaned over the edge of the bridge to paint several huge stencils. The bridge is just a few hundred feet from the ancient meeting ground of the Mespat Indians.

New York is a galaxy of adventure at once elegant, exciting, and bizarre. It's a city that moves so fast, it takes energy just to stand still.

— Barbara Walters, TV interviewer

## Animal House

A Bronx fire station proudly calls itself "Animal House," and was at the center of a sex scandal that resulted in the suspension of two firefighters and the reassignment of 14 others. This all occurred after a romp with a self-proclaimed fireman groupie. The Staten Island woman first reported that she had been raped, but later told police that she had had consensual sex with four firefighters, and that she has had sex with 200-300 firefighters since 9/11. She said she suffers from herpes—and bipolar disorder.

## Doesn't Get Out Much

A man in his 50s was found dead in his upscale Manhattan apartment. The doorman said that the man hadn't been out of his apartment in 13 years and that he had everything delivered. An employee of a restaurant in the next block said the man had been calling for the same meal three times a day every day for eight years: rice pudding, chicken soup, two eggs over easy, sausages, cheesecake. A neighbor said that the man used to be in the adult entertainment business.

> The doorman said that the man hadn't been out of his apartment in 13 years.

## Whistle Blower

A Riker's Island corrections officer had one fight too many with his wife, having thrown her out of the family car on the way home from a party. The next day while he was at work, his wife called the cops and blew the whistle on him. She showed them the information stored on his computer, which she knew contained child pornography.

## Corpse Care

A couple in the Bronx forced their foster child to continue to care for a corpse. The girl was made to conceal the man's death because she was afraid of being removed from the home. The couple was indicted on charges of child abuse and elder neglect, relating to the woman's elderly father who suffered from Alzheimer's disease and lived in the house with them. He died, but his body was never removed and the girl was told to bring him meals. It was the stench that finally got neighbors to call the authorities.

## Signed, Sealed, Delivered

A young man of 25 from Brooklyn had four weeks of vacation coming so he decided to visit his parents in a suburb of Dallas, Texas. Rather than buy a plane ticket for $320, the man, a shipping clerk, packed himself into a shipping crate and air-expressed himself home, charging the $550 freight charge to his employer. Before setting out, he filled out shipping instructions stating the crate held a computer and clothes. A friend helped to load him in and close the crate. The young man, Charles D. McKinley, was 5'8" tall and weighed 170 pounds. He squeezed himself into a crate that measured 42 by 36 by 15 inches. The crate was taken by truck from New York's Kennedy Airport to New Jersey, where it was loaded onto a heated, pressurized cargo plane. Since air cargo planes are believed to receive less security attention than passenger planes because of the sheer volume that they carry, his presence in the crate got through security undetected. The trip took 15 hours, going from Newark, New Jersey's airport to Niagara Falls, New York, on to the carrier's hub in Fort Wayne, Indiana, and on to Dallas. During the journey, McKinley was able to get out of the crate a few times to stretch his legs, before maneuvering himself back in and closing the crate.

In Dallas, a driver for Pilot Air Freight picked up the crate and delivered it to McKinley's parents' home in suburban DeSota. When the crate was delivered to his parents' door, he pushed himself out of the box in front of an eyewitness: the delivery driver, who immediately called the police. After an investigation by the FBI and many other federal officers and administrators, the young man was charged as a stowaway, a federal misdemeanor. However, since McKinley was wanted in New York for unrelated traffic charges, jail may be the next cramped abode in his future.

## It Doesn't Get Much Stranger Than This...

In the first half of the 20th century two brothers lived in New York called Homer and Langley Collyer. They were recluses, living in a booby-trapped, junk-stuffed, newspaper-packed brownstone house until they died mysteriously in 1947.

The Collyers moved into their home at Fifth Avenue and 128th Street in 1909. Homer, the older brother, worked as an attorney while Langley earned his living as a concert pianist. Throughout their lives, no one was allowed onto the premises. They had no gas, electricity, or any other modern convenience of the time. In 1932, Homer had a stroke that left him bedridden and blind, and Langley stayed even closer to home, venturing out only to buy groceries.

According to reports, Langley once explained that he kept thousands of old newspapers in the house because he believed Homer would want to read them when he regained his sight. And the reason for having 14 grand pianos in the house was because Homer liked to hear his brother play.

Few knew anything about the two recluses until March 21, 1947, when the police received a strange telephone call from an unidentified caller saying that Homer "was no more" and giving the police the address. The police went to the house, but no one answered. They tried to break in with no success. Firemen came and used axes, but still couldn't get in; something was blocking their way. Finally, they forced open a second-story shutter.

When they went downstairs, the police and firemen realized the front door had been blocked by thousands of neatly bundled stacks of newspapers. Inside the house on Fifth Avenue the police found Homer Collyer in a gray bathrobe, sitting straight up in a chair. But no brother.

For the next two weeks, authorities cleaned out an estimated 120 tons of debris, including the aforementioned pianos, newspapers, a Model-T Ford automobile—and all the rats that infested the place. The house was like a maze, with tiny passages created between towers of stacked books, boxes, and papers, some of which had been rigged with wire and bucket booby traps.

On April 8, Langley was finally found, only 10 feet from his brother. Langley was decomposing under a mammoth stack of newspapers that had been booby trapped. Langley had died of heart failure after the trap had somehow gone wrong, and a suitcase, three breadboxes, and several bundles of newspapers fell on him. Langley died first, it turned out, and Homer a few days later, from starvation.

When they died, the brothers had an estate worth $300,000. Where the money ultimately went, no one has ever learned.

## Sword Swallowing

In New York City on November 11, 1817, Senaa Samma gave the nation's first exhibition of sword swallowing.

## The Players

John Wilkes Booth's brother, Edwin Booth, founded The Players in 1888, a club for actors located in Gramercy Park.

## Self-Service Sculpting

New York has more than its share of unappreciated and unrecognized artists. Sculptors have created their own self-service exhibition site in Queens where they can display their work.

## Corpse From the Crypt

Three students in New York City were accused of a taking a corpse from a crypt. They dressed it as Darth Vader, the *Star Wars*' villain, and took it to a fancy dress party.

## A Real Bargain

The owner of the Abracadabra Superstore has instituted a new policy of rounding down—for example, a shopper pays only $32 on a $32.75 bill. The store owner said he started the policy because he was "getting lazy and too old" to go to the bank for change. He claims the rule has kept customers from asking for discounts. This policy is believed to be the first for any retailer anywhere in the United States.

## Corporate Gas

Two entrepreneurial authors have put a new spin on climbing the corporate ladder. A new book called *Going Corporate: Moving Up Without Screwing Up* by Brad Embree and Jared Shapiro suggests that passing gas tells a lot about who you are and who you want to be. You're really in the know, they suggest, if you "let one fly" in the copy room because it's well ventilated from the heat generated by the equipment, thus minimizing your trail. Learning the etiquette of things that seem unimportant, they believe, enhances what they call your "promotional potential."

## Thrill Seeker

A performance artist's show in New York City consisted of him putting on headgear and boxing gloves, and then inviting audience members to try to knock him out. Anyone who was successful would be awarded a prize of $1,000. Several people walked off with money. Fifteen years ago, this same danger-loving performance artist jumped off a five-story building onto a tiny cushion, just to experience the thrill of his life being threatened.

## They Don't Make Teachers Like They Used To

A top-ranking New York City school official pleaded guilty recently to forgery after investigators found that she had created a totally fictitious background using documents she had stolen from a friend.

For over 20 years, Joan Mahon-Powell climbed the ranks all the way from a one-time Brooklyn substitute teacher (and there is doubt she even had the credentials to do that), to full salaried teacher, who was demoted back to being a substitute when officials discovered she was not a certified teacher.

That didn't stop other officials in the New York City school system from appointing her acting assistant principal of a Brooklyn school, then promoting her first to principal, then acting superintendent of a school district, then top aide to the chancellor, and more promotions until she was earning $152,500 a year.

> Mahon-Powell's life began to fall apart when she was asked to submit her credentials.

Mahon-Powell's life began to fall apart when, during a routine review while serving in her latest post as instructional superintendent of a Brooklyn school district, she was asked to submit her credentials. It turned out that all the paperwork actually belonged to a retired administrator in the school system and Mahon-Powell's best friend.

Although charged with fraud, she did not have to serve any jail time. The question remained, however, over how could she have risen so high in the system, even after it was discovered early in her career that she was not licensed to teach. One has to wonder what she really taught in her classes, and if maybe

New York City school administrators might want to go back and take a course themselves, on how to tell a cheat from a fake.

## Paint It Black

A Queens teenager was questioned by her school principal about her style of clothing and makeup, known as Goth. She explained that Goths are basically miserable all the time, and the most interesting people are always the saddest. She told the principal she was happy being so sad.

## Barbie in the Bronx

There was a man who checked himself into a Bronx hospital complaining of severe abdominal pain. His vital signs were normal, but the X-rays showed several Barbie doll heads lodged in his small bowel. He deliberately swallowed them because he found the sensation of excreting them pleasurable.

## Crash and Burn

A young man was found speeding early in the morning on the Brooklyn-Queens Expressway. He passed several cars illegally, eventually lost control of the car, crashed, and died. The boy's parents decided to file a lawsuit against the last driver his son illegally passed, who they claimed had veered to the left, causing their son to leave the road and crash. The case was settled out of court.

## Business As Unusual

Brock Enright, a 25-year-old artist, has created a business where New Yorkers pay him thousands of dollars to be abducted. This is called "designer kidnapping" and has become the ultimate thrill for jaded New Yorkers.

Each kidnapping is different, customized to the client's particular tastes and needs. Invariably, most of them are bound and gagged, taken away, and "held hostage" for a period of time that could last for hours or even days, depending on the client's wishes. One young man, a carpenter, has enjoyed a kidnap experience three times because, as he has said, "It's about stepping outside of yourself."

Many clients are abducted in the street, day or night. Some are awakened at home during the night by Mr. Enright's operatives, or "birds" as he calls them. The kidnap victim agrees on a time frame for the abduction, but part of the thrill is not knowing exactly when the birds will swoop down and strike. Some psychotherapists believe there may be therapeutic value to these fake, fun kidnappings in that they reinforce the sense of satisfaction and accomplishment that comes from surviving a terrible ordeal.

There is nothing illegal about this business, although it isn't exactly something the New York City Police Department endorses. What is particularly interesting, but not surprising given that this exists in New York City, is that in the various cases that have occurred on city streets, no one has intervened to help the so-called victim.

It can destroy an individual, or it can fulfill him, depending a good deal on luck. No one should come to New York to live unless he is willing to be lucky.

–E.B. White, *Here Is New York*, 1949

## Bullet in the Head

Doctors for a New York City writer saw that the man's CAT scan revealed he had a bullet in his head—to their and the man's utter surprise. Searching his memory, the man vaguely recalled an incident of almost 30 years ago when he wandered too close to a fight on a loading dock, heard a noise, and was knocked down. He remembered staggering home, somewhat bloody, but went to bed without seeking medical attention because the bleeding had stopped. It would be too dangerous now, the doctors say, to remove the bullet, which remains in his head.

### Faker Quaker

There is a Quaker cemetery in Prospect Park in Brooklyn. Oddly enough given his rather un-Quaker-like existence, the actor Montgomery Clift—whom Marilyn Monroe said was "the only person in worse shape than I am"—was laid to rest there in 1966.

## Flashmobbing

New Yorkers are seriously into a new experience called "flashmobbing." Flash mobs are not-so-random crowds—coordinated via the Internet—who gather in a predetermined location, perform some brief action, and then quickly disperse. To protect the pleasure to be derived from each event, participants aren't told exactly what the mob is supposed to do until just before the event happens. For instance, for one recent happening, participants passed around an e-mail telling them to assemble at the food court in Grand Central Station where organizers—identified by a copy of a magazine they were holding—gave the mobbers printed instructions on what they were to do next. The action they were told to do was assemble suddenly on the mezzanine level of the Grand Hyatt Hotel next to Grand Central Station, applaud loudly for 15 seconds, and then leave. About 200 flash mobbers did exactly that.

A similar episode happened at a carpet store in Manhattan when a huge crowd inexplicably gathered around a particular rug. The flash mobbers told the salespeople that they all lived together in a warehouse in Queens and were thinking of buying a rug. The crowd dispersed after exactly 10 minutes.

Then there was the incident of a mob of 200 or so meeting in Central Park near the Museum of Natural History to imitate birds and chant the word "nature" before quietly going their separate ways. Although now prevalent in London, Berlin, Vienna, and Zurich, New York is, not surprisingly, the birthplace of flashmobbing which has been called, by turns, installation art, cultural critique, anthropological experiment—and an excuse to do something different.

## Cuddle Up

Another new craze created by two New Yorkers is the "cuddle party" which invites people to pay $30 each to touch and embrace others in an intimate gathering, everyone wearing pajamas—but no sex allowed. Everyone needs to be cuddled, especially in lonely New York, say the two entrepreneurs, and this is a good, safe way to meet new and interesting people. And in case things get too steamy, there's a small chime that is rung to break up the action, if necessary.

The idea for cuddle parties came about after one of the creators, a masseur, began giving massages to other masseurs who never got a chance to get their own massage. One day he noticed a woman crying hysterically from the emotional release brought on by her massage.

Before any touching begins, participants—all of whom are wearing pajamas— gather in a circle to hear the rules and voice any questions or concerns. Then the participants team up into pairs, and to ensure that the boundaries of what is permissible are clear, they practice saying "no" to the question, "May I kiss you?" Cuddling 101 begins by hugging three people. People then get in a circle on their hands and knees, rub shoulders, and moo like cows. After a bit of swaying back and forth, everyone falls to one side, putting them in an easy cuddling position.

Cuddle parties are intended for people who are emotionally "sound." People in therapy or who are seeing a mental health professional are asked to consult their doctor before signing up for a party and to tell the organizers of their situation.

New York is the only city in the world where you can get deliberately run down on the sidewalk by a pedestrian.

— Russell Baker, *New York Times* columnist

## Dead Giveaway

Police arrested a burglar after finding his shorts and wallet in the front yard of the Staten Island house that he had burglarized. According to police reports, he entered the house early in the morning in his underwear, burgled it, then left. When the residents called the police, the officers found the thief's clothing in the front yard, and, of course, in his wallet was his driver's license, the perfect I.D.

## Caught Red-Handed

In Queens, at a White Castle restaurant located next to a bank, police arrested a bank robbery suspect before he could take one bite of his burger. The suspect had passed a teller at the bank a note demanding money, then fled through a back exit with an undisclosed amount. A police officer checking area businesses was told that someone had left clothing, matching a description of what the robber wore, in the restaurant's restroom. The officer found the thief at the condiment counter, in the clothes he had worn underneath the ones he had removed. And he was carrying the loot from the bank in his pockets and in a plastic bag from the local supermarket.

## Prayers at Prospect Lake

A Brooklyn man stormed into the administration offices of Prospect Park, demanding to be compensated for carving tools that had been stolen while he was in the park carving up tree stumps—without official permission. It turns out that the man was both an artist and a community leader, and he was creating Haitian folk art, working on tree stumps near Prospect Lake. Although not officially sanctioned as an altar, the site has become a place for a variety of religious observances from Buddhists throwing goldfish into the pond to Muslims celebrating the end of Ramadan.

## Monkey Business

Orlando Lopez was a veterinary clinic technician who decided to turn his Manhattan apartment into his own personal zoo. Animal control officers confiscated—or rescued—six monkeys, a Great Dane, a Chihuahua, two cats, and a tarantula named Fang from his Washington Heights studio apartment. The only pets Lopez was allowed to keep were some fish.

Lopez and his roommate slept in the kitchen while their animals had the main room to themselves. There were also three, five-by-four-foot wrought-iron cages specially equipped so the monkeys could swing in them. The monkeys—Mandy, Michael, Marley, Chucky, Lulu, and Belle—were a mixed variety. There were two capuchins, two marmosets, and two squirrel monkeys, and at least two of them seemed to dread being separated from Lopez as they clung to him while the animal control officers tried to get them.

The pets had been living in the apartment for four years, and neighbors had repeatedly complained about the smell of urine seeping into the halls. However, no one ever complained because the monkeys, weighing one to five pounds, and ranging in age from three to nine years old, never caused a ruckus that disturbed the neighbors, although they did like to switch the apartment lights on and off and pull the cats' tails.

Lopez said his monkeys liked to watch TV and listen to the radio, especially a show called the *Morning Zoo*.

## New York Super Heroes

Stan Lee and Jack Kirby are the creators of many Marvel Comics superheroes. They were both born in New York, and Marvel's offices are in Manhattan so, as a result, many characters live there too. Spider-Man lives in Forest Hills, Queens; the Fantastic Four live at the fictitious Four Freedoms Plaza in midtown east of Manhattan; Daredevil lives in Hell's Kitchen. Then there are the Avengers who own a mansion at 890 Fifth Avenue which, if a real address, would be on the site of the actual Frick Museum. Dr. Strange, Earth's Sorcerer Supreme, resides at a non-existent number on Bleecker Street in Greenwich Village.

## Backwards Mile Race

For athletes who like to see where they've been instead of where they're going, they can participate in the Backwards Mile Race held every April Fool's Day in Central Park.

## Bite of the Apple

In the five boroughs of New York City people bite around 1,500 other people a year.

## Shell Society

There are 2,000 members in the New York Turtle and Tortoise Society.

# It Takes All Kinds of Animal Lovers

In Union Square Park in Manhattan, there are strange little boxes in some of the trees that are not for birds. They are the result of one man's affection for squirrels. A retired handyman had been coming to feed the squirrels in Union Square for years; in fact, decades ago when he arrived here from Cuba. He found the fuzzy nut-eaters so enchanting that he decided to build a shelter for pregnant squirrels so they'd have a safe haven in which to breed.

He put together eight boxes from scrap wood, bored an entryway into each one, stuffed them with shredded newspaper, and mounted them in the forks of trees around Union Square Park. Needless to say, urban squirrels are a hardy bunch, but they knew a good thing when they saw one, and gravitated to their new habitats with little encouragement needed.

For a while, everything seemed fine, but then one hot summer morning, the creature-caring handyman discovered that his shelters had been dismantled and removed. After repeated letters to the park's commissioner, the handyman was given permission to reconstruct his squirrel homes, which he still visits twice a day.

# Blind, Bearded, and Beloved

For almost three decades, at the corner of Sixth Avenue and 54th Street, stood a man who came to be known as Moondog. The son of an itinerant minister, Louis T. Hardin was born in Kansas in 1916. He was blinded in 1932 when a dynamite cap exploded in his hands. He then began studying musical composition at the Iowa School for the Blind, and came to New York in 1943 to study music.

By 1947, he had found his post at Sixth Avenue and 54th Street, close to his beloved Carnegie Hall where he would go to listen to rehearsals. Dressed in a self-made leather and fur Viking costume with helmet and spear, and a full, Viking-type beard, he called himself Moondog and sold sheet music and poetry on the street, and played instruments of his own invention, depending upon the charity donations of passers-by.

Eventually, his skills as a composer claimed the attention of some music industry professionals and he began to record his music. He has been hailed by such highly regarded musicians as Charlie Parker and Philip Glass. In 1974, Moondog was invited to tour West Germany where he still resides with his wife whom he met there and who put away his spear and helmet for good. Many of his old recordings have been re-released on CD and are available today.

## Pet Pigeons

The New York City Health Department found 60 pigeons in one man's townhouse in the extremely posh neighborhood of 77th Street and Fifth Avenue. He allowed the birds to fly free and roam about in three of the five stories of his building. The Health Department found that he had not committed any violation. The man spends approximately $20,000 caring for the pigeons and other pets.

## Club Stats

There are 150 people in the Queens Psychic Club and several of them visit the Vampire Institute located in Queens. Only 30 people are in New York City's Barbie and Ken Doll Collector's Club.

## Art of Tattooing

Mechanical tattooing was invented by a barber in 1899 in his Chatham Square shop. Samuel F. O'Reilly adapted the ink tube and tip of Thomas Edison's new electric engraving pen. He became so successful that he stopped giving shaves and haircuts, and turned his shop into America's first tattoo parlor.

## Hearse Tour

Paul Bearer takes tourists around to spots in New York City that are part of his "Lifestyles of the Rich and Dead" tour. He drives people around in his hearse.

## The Turk

The National Hotel once existed on Broadway between Pine and Cedar streets downtown. There, on April 13, 1826, a man by the name of Johann Maelzel and his invention, "The Turk" made their American debut. "The Turk" was a chess machine. He wore a turban, and was made of wood with a "body" of gears, wheels, cogs, and metal parts that whirred and whirled. He sat in front of a large box with a chess board on top. According to Maelzel, "The Turk" had been amazing European audiences and had even played a game of chess with Napoleon and won.

Americans were thrilled and amazed, too, until Maelzel's hoax was revealed. Hidden within the box was a small but skilled chess player who operated "The Turk." This hidden "brain" managed to fool audiences by cleverly moving between inner compartments just before Maelzel would open a series of doors exposing "The Turk's" mechanical workings and proving to his gullible audiences that "The Turk" was pure machine.

## Under Spiritual Ride

At 434 Broadway stood Barnum's Hotel, where Margaret Fox and her sister Kate dazzled New Yorkers in the summer of 1850. The Fox sisters launched the spiritualism movement in America, and that summer, they held their mysterious "rapping" séances at Barnum's. They charged one dollar and people flocked to their performances. Noted editor Horace Greeley was just one of many supposedly bright people who was totally convinced of their powers, and in his paper, *The Tribune*, he regaled his readers with evidence of the sisters' gifts. Almost 40 years later, Margaret finally confessed her longtime hoax. Rather than messages from the "other side," she  admitted that she produced the rappings by cracking her knuckles.

## Fraudster Comes Good

William Sydney Porter had been serving time for bank fraud in an Ohio prison. When he was released in 1902, he came to New York City and stayed at a hotel on West 24th Street. Given his less than stellar background, he decided to start fresh, even changing his name. He took the pseudonym O. Henry, and began to write the wonderful short stories that are still being read today.

## Bullfight

In 1880, Angel Fernandez built the Central Park Arena at West 116th Street and Lenox Avenue. It was Manhattan's only bullring with seating for 10,000. During that summer, eight toreadors performed three bullfights with untamed steers shipped from Texas. Angel closed down the spectacle after the first summer.

## Secret Agent

Rudolf Abel was born in England, and lived in Brooklyn from 1950 to 1962. During that time he coordinated the activities of a number of spies for the Soviet Union, since he was a career intelligence officer for the Russians. He used the name Emil R. Golfus and worked out of an art and photography studio. Eventually the FBI found out about him, and during a search of his home found spy equipment, including a shortwave transmitter and receiver which he used to communicate with Moscow.

In 1957, he was sentenced to 30 years in prison, and then, in 1962, he was sent to the Soviet Union in exchange for Francis Gary Powers, the pilot of an American reconnaissance plane who had been shot down over Russia.

## A Sour Taste in the Mouth

A woman took herself to a clinic in Brooklyn after eating three birth-control vaginal inserts. A recent émigré from Russia, her English was so bad that she had to draw a picture. The doctor still wasn't sure what she was saying, or drawing, and finally a translator appeared who explained that the woman thought the inserts were some kind of candy or gum because she could not read the words in English on the foil wrappers. After the third one, when her throat and mouth began to fill with a sour-tasting foam, she took herself to the clinic.

## The Greatest Showman—or Con Man—of Them All

Phineas Taylor Barnum was born in Connecticut in 1810. In 1841, he took over the defunct Scudder's Museum at Broadway and Ann Street, and opened the American Museum. A brilliant promoter and an ardent believer in the gullibility of people, P. T. Barnum's American Museum was the most successful of the many "dime" museums anywhere. Here he presented performances by the midget Charles Stratton, aka General Tom Thumb, and even claimed he had a genuine "Fejee mermaid." He put on baby contests, melodramas, poultry shows, and curiosities of the natural world, providing inexpensive entertainment. Today, the three-ring circus that bears his name is all glitter and glamour and is anything but inexpensive—but as he said, there's always some sucker ready to buy.

### Fence Fool

Ten-year-old Dimitri Michel was climbing a wrought-iron fence on his way to visit a friend in the Flatbush section of Brooklyn when he slipped and impaled his arm on a four-inch post. The spike was sticking up through his arm and he was just hanging there, dangling until firefighters and an EMS crew arrived and took him to the hospital. Dimitri obviously doesn't learn from his mistakes. He impaled the same arm two years earlier doing the exact same fence climbing.

## Swimming the Hudson

After every 20 minutes that Christopher Swain spent swimming in the Hudson River, he gargled with hydrogen peroxide to protect himself from swallowing any toxic chemicals. His plan was to swim the entire 315-mile stretch of the river, costing him about $19,000, which included the price of goggles, wet suits, and a 12-foot manned boat to follow him. He swam the Hudson to encourage corporations, governments, and residents to make the river cleaner. He vaccinated himself to protect against hepatitis, tetanus, and typhoid as he swam from New York state's highest peak, Mount Marcy, to the Verrazano Narrows Bridge in the city. He swam about six hours a day for 35 days, taking breaks to plead his position in communities along the way, and completed his journey in July 2004.

## Food for Thought

Cosimo Cavallaro is unique among New York City artists. He once repainted a New York City hotel room in melted mozzarella. Another work was an installation in a street-level gallery of a midtown Manhattan hotel that involved slicing 312 pounds of ham and tossing the meat on top of a four-poster bed. The installation took three and a half hours, and was kept fresh for two days thanks to air conditioning. He also welcomes cockroaches and other bugs to his food installations, believing they are part of the artist's palette.

## Licking Her Boots

A Columbia University student was arrested for sexual abuse. He sneaked into a female classmate's room while she was sleeping and began to lick her feet. When she awoke, he allegedly held her down and molested her. She was too scared to report the incident until a second attack of toe-kissing foreplay was reported.

## Garbology

A. J. Weberman is the world's self-proclaimed expert on Bob Dylan. He got this way by going through Dylan's garbage when the singer-songwriter lived in Greenwich Village, giving rise to the term "garbology" or the art of going through a celebrity's trash to gather information.

## Defrauding Dermatologist

For years, Dr. Jonathan Zizmor was known as the subway dermatologist. His self-designed ads were on every subway car in the 1970s and 1980s, advertising his skill and rates to rid one of acne and other unsightly skin conditions. Recently, Dr. Zizmor was charged with fraud for billing $100,000 for a procedure that he never performed. He was also fined and put on probation—no more ads for the subway zitmeister—for failing to perform adequate histories and physical examinations on nine patients, four of whom were undercover agents.

## Crime of Passion

Sol Wachtler was the chief judge of New York State's highest court, the Court of Appeals, and seemed next in line to be governor when he was arrested by the FBI in 1992 for extortion, demanding money, and threatening the lives of his ex-lover and step-cousin, socialite Joy Silverman and her daughter. After Silverman broke up with him, he was desolate, acting the cool judge while masking the turmoil within. Wachtler posed as a private investigator and sent vulgar, threatening letters to her. She enlisted the FBI. Wachtler, one of the most respected judges in New York, was sentenced to 15 months in prison for extortion and sexual harassment.

### The Strange Tale of the Cat Lady

It is said that beauty is in the eye of the beholder. If that is true, then New York socialite Jocelyne Wildenstein needs new glasses. Dubbed "Tiger Woman," Wildenstein is considered a peer without equal among New York City's oddballs.

Jocelyne was a very beautiful young woman from a middle class family in Lausanne, Switzerland. An ambitious woman who wanted more from life than marriage and a family in Lausanne, Jocelyne believed that her looks would be her ticket out. She became both a skilled hunter and a pilot of small planes, which brought her an invitation to a shooting weekend at the 66,000-acre Kenyan estate of Alec Wildenstein, heir to a $10 billion art fortune. Scandal had followed the Wildenstein family since World War II. Jewish, they had been accused of both buying and selling art from the Nazis during the war. Alec was enchanted by Jocelyn's Nordic good looks as well as her lion hunting ability. He invited her for a motorcycle ride through his estate and the sexual attraction was immediate and strong. Within a year, they were married in a lavish Las Vegas ceremony, and then they moved into his spacious Park Avenue apartment. Jocelyne felt as if her every dream had been fulfilled.

While Alec managed the art business, Jocelyne learned to become a Park Avenue socialite, as well as mistress of the Wildenstein's various homes including a Caribbean beach estate, a chateau in France, and a house she had him buy in Lausanne. They traveled everywhere in his private jet. Their New York townhouse was five stories and had an indoor swimming pool. Always loving exotic animals, Alec bought his bride a rare monkey as a household pet, even though having a monkey as a pet is illegal in New York. They also had five purebred greyhounds.

Then there were the clothes and the jewels, of course. Her jewelry collection was valued in excess of $10 million. And in exchange, Jocelyne gave Alec two children. But as the years wore on, the marriage became less than perfect, as often happens, but when it happens with the very rich, it's different.

Alec resented the control his father still exerted over him and the business. The only pleasures that Alec seemed to take in life were his exquisite art collection and the lions in his private jungle in Kenya. Jocelyne felt insecure and jealous, especially when her husband's eye started to wander.

Pushing fifty, growing more and more insecure about the loss of her looks, her one calling card in life, and deeply concerned about the loss of her husband's affections, Jocelyne knew drastic measures were called for. She visited a renowned New York City plastic surgeon who was also a friend of the family. She loved Alec and wanted to please him. Regaining her beautiful, young looks would do just that.

*No one has been able to determine how many surgeries she has had.*

The first few surgeries—a nip here, a tuck there—were so successful that Alec decided to have a little work done on himself. Things were good again… until she discovered that Alec was sleeping with other women.

Jocelyne knew that Alec loved his jungle estate and the cats that inhabited it, probably more than anything else in life including his children or even his art collection. Desperate, Jocelyne returned to her plastic surgeon and instructed him to make her look like one of Alec's beloved cats. Though the request was unorthodox, the surgeon complied.

No one has ever been able to determine exactly how many surgeries Jocelyne Wildenstein has had, there may have been too many to keep track of.

But from a very beautiful, albeit aging, woman she became a laughing stock, "the queen of the jungle" who was featured in magazines and on television for the grotesque mess she had made of her face. Her lips were abnormally thickened and her eyes pulled back so extremely as to form a cat-eye effect. She even underwent skin darkening treatments.

Alec began divorce proceedings, which was not the effect Jocelyne had wanted. She went back again to the plastic surgeon, and to other plastic surgeons to do anything to hold on to this man—and the lifestyle. During the divorce proceedings, Jocelyne entered their townhouse once to find a strange woman in a towel and her husband pointing a gun and threatening to kill Jocelyne. Charges were filed. Jocelyne sued Alec for a $200 million settlement, as well as millions and millions in art, homes, and a $200,000 a month allowance. Alec countered by reducing her staff of seven to one, reducing use of the jet, and removing her pet monkey.

The divorce was eventually granted, and Jocelyne received tens of millions of dollars while Alec went off with his Russian model girlfriend. But as it turned out, neither Alec nor Jocelyne were happy without the other. Although she may have gone overboard to be his cat lady, and even though he had not been supportive of her as a proper husband should be, the two really loved each other, and they are together again, the cat lady and her tamer.

# PART V:
# Only in New York

*New York is a sucked orange.*

— Ralph Waldo Emerson

*New York is a great city to live in if you can afford to get out of it.*

— William Cole, author, 1992

Every place, whether a tiny rural village or a tourist destination, has its history, its oddballs, its criminals, its legends. What New York City offers is not so much unique but larger than life, beyond belief. From the beginning of its discovery and development, it is always the diversity of its population that has allowed and encouraged life to be lived in New York as in no other place on earth. A willingness to explore, experiment, and experience is the hallmark of the true New Yorker. They do not take "no" easily. Rules and regulations are as difficult to enforce here as in any jungle. New Yorkers do not think they are above the law; they just think they know better and are better than people anywhere else. And it is this kind of hubris that makes others dislike New Yorkers even when they admire that same arrogance. Day in and day out, just struggling with the mass of humanity, the lack of light, the crowd of buildings, the sounds of construction, the services that don't work, the prices that are obscene, the yawning disparity between the haves and have-nots, the similarly gaping disparity between Manhattan and the rest of New York City creates events, achievements, and people that could only happen in New York. (Although Brooklyn is getting very, very close to being as rude and inconsiderate, as well as being just as expensive.)

Weird, strange, exciting, incredible, unbelievable, laughable—New York City is a breeding ground and a safe haven for the people and happenings that can be described as all of this and more. There are those who would leave New York only as a sailor takes shore leave, desperate to return to his ship. There are those who come to New York with dreams so ridiculous, with no possible wherewithal or common sense to achieve them, that they leave cursing the city for being uninhabitable by decent folk. There are those who live in New York insulated from the real world, their money protecting them from the reality of subways, bank lines, the ordinary people living ordinary lives. And then there is everyone else: the immigrants from Jamaica and Ethiopia and Mexico and Guatemala and Pakistan; the college graduate from the Corn Belt and the student from the suburbs; the wannabe actress, musician, dancer, or comic; the business school graduate with Wall Street dollar-sign dreams; the Koreans and the Russians who find freedom and build empires of nail salons and small groceries. From Staten Island to Queens, Brooklyn, the Bronx, and Manhattan, New York can house anyone, but be home to very few. This is a city that will not meet you halfway; all the effort has to come from you. For those who try, most of the time it is worth it. But sometimes things happen here that are so unique to the city and its character that one can say, "Only in New York" and everyone will know exactly what you mean.

## Change of Name

The Clarion Hotel Fifth Avenue in Manhattan recently changed its name to Hotel 5A which executives say is an abbreviation for Fifth Avenue and is meant to sound like a typical New York apartment number. To celebrate, the hotel is offering a free night to anyone who can prove they've legally changed their name. Name changes due to marriage or divorce do not count. No one has stepped forward to claim the free room.

## Germs on the Subway

Anthrax analysis of swabs taken in the New York City subway system took longer than planned because of the unexpectedly high amount of other bacteria.

## Tiger Tales

New York City animal control officers managed to capture a 425-pound tiger after shooting it with a tranquilizer gun. The tiger resided in Antoine Yates' fifth floor apartment at a Harlem housing project; he'd had the tiger since it was a cub.

> The tiger resided in Antoine Yates' fifth floor apartment at a Harlem housing project.

Officers also removed a five-foot-long alligator from the apartment. Police tracked Yates down to a Philadelphia hospital where he was being treated for animal bites.

## Wig Out

Some visitors to Coney Island were trapped on the roller coaster for 30 minutes when someone's wig blew off and caught in the wheels, and the cars ground to a halt at the top of the climb. The ride continued after rescue workers removed a brown wig that had gotten tangled up under one of the cars. The rollercoaster manager was not surprised since things often fly out from the cars during the ride, although usually it's a sweater, not a wig.

## Cell Phone Jam

New York City passengers experienced major delays during the evening rush hour commute when a man got his arm stuck in the toilet of a Metro-North train while trying to retrieve his dropped cell phone. Train traffic was tied up for 90 minutes while firefighters struggled to free the man, a task which ultimately required disassembling the toilet *in situ*. The phone was not recovered.

## Empty Art

"The Empty Museum" installation by two New York City artists consisted only of four walls, representing the walls of a 19th-century art gallery with nothing on them. It was well-reviewed and well-received.

## Yoga for Dogs

The yoga pose, "Downward Facing Dog," is now being offered—to dogs. At a park in New York City, "Ruff Yoga" classes are being held. These are a series of 45-minute yoga poses owners can do with their dogs. The human students start in a seated position with their dogs on their laps. The humans chant "ohm"—and some dogs have been known to respond to this sound with a gentle howl of their own. From the sitting position, the two-leggeds and the four-leggeds do stretches, headstands, and back bends. These canine classes are free—for the dog.

## Time for a Little Nap

On the 24th floor of the Empire State Building, two enterprising entrepreneurs have established MetroNaps, a lounge offering harried New Yorkers a 20-minute power nap to re-energize themselves for life in the Big Apple. Customers are seated in a futuristic chair or "napping pod" in a quiet, darkened room. The nappers stretch out in reclining seats, with blankets covering their legs and music piped into headphones. Fourteen dollars and 20 minutes later, the sleeping pod wakes up the customer with a combination of vibrations and light. The MetroNap pods, which are like plush dentist's chairs, cost $8,000 each and are now being sold separately. They may be seen soon at airport lounges for busy executives, who fancy a nap before their flight.

### New York Minute

Anti-stress candy has been created just for New York. Its slogan is: "Relax in a New York minute"—meaning in one minute, expect the candy to work wonders. The term New York minute refers to the fact that New York City is very busy. Much is happening at all hours of the day and night, people are often in a hurry and can be impatient, so it really implies a period of time much shorter than a minute.

## Fresh Milk

Milk cartons sold outside the five boroughs supposedly have two expiration dates: one dated three days earlier specifically designated for New York City.

Everywhere outside New York City is Bridgeport, Connecticut.

– Fred Allen, radio comedian

When you leave New York, you ain't goin' nowhere.

– Anonymous

## Museum of Sex

Opened in 2002, the Museum of Sex on Fifth Avenue and 27th Street was the first of its kind in North America. Its mission is to preserve and present the history, evolution, and cultural significance of human sexuality. Its inaugural exhibition was: *NYC Sex: How New York City Transformed Sex in America.* The museum contains a detailed history of the city's sexual subcultures from 1825 to the present, and holds classes such as the art of burlesque.

## Dirty Sole

There are more bacteria on the sole of a single New York City shoe than there are people in the entire country of Gambia.

## Sidewalk Rage

Diagonal walking accounts for 77 percent of all sidewalk rage incidents.

## Fresh Kills

For a time, the world's largest garbage dump, at 2,200 acres, was Fresh Kills on Staten Island. Approximately 10,300 tons of residential and institutional waste are produced in New York City each day, which is down from the 16,000 tons accumulated daily before the city began to recycle in 1993. The dump was closed in Spring 2001 but was used as the main site for depositing the debris from the World Trade Center Towers after 9/11. There are plans to possibly turn it into a memorial park.

## Pick Up Your Poop

Before the enactment of the 1978 law making it mandatory for dog owners in New York City to clean up after their pets, approximately 40 million pounds of poop was deposited on the streets each year.

## Subway Assistance

A green globe outside a subway entrance means it is manned 24 hours a day. A red globe means the entrance is closed or unavailable.

## Borough of Churches

Brooklyn's nickname is the Borough of Churches because it has 725 of them. One of them, Our Lady of Lebanon on Remsen Street, is embedded with a fragment of Plymouth Rock. The nickname of Queens is the Borough of Homes.

## Queen's Country Fair

Every September is time for the Queen's Country Fair at New York City's only working farm. It has all the trimmings of a real country fair, with livestock raising competitions, pie-eating contests, and even pig racing. There are carnival rides, hayrides, and a two-acre cornfield maze.

## Opera Lovers

Former Manhattan mayors Fiorello LaGuardia and Rudolph Giuliani liked to exercise their Italian musical heritage. LaGuardia conducted bands and orchestras, and Giuliani did walk-ons at the Metropolitan Opera.

## A New York State of Mind

There is a billboard in Times Square advertising the Swatch watch company. Two cartoon bunnies are featured on a new watch that utilizes touch crystal technology. Touching the watch face causes the hands to spin wildly and come to rest in different positions before returning to the actual time. The maneuvers of the two cartoon bunnies occasionally result in a somewhat intimate position, and are now called the "Bunnysutra."

### You Can't Make an Omelet

At a New York City hotel restaurant, there is an omelet on the menu made of eggs, caviar, lobster, and a few other delicacies. The price for the omelet is $1,000. It has six eggs and 10 ounces of sevruga caviar which the restaurant pays $65 an ounce for. A budget version of the omelet, with only one ounce of caviar, sells for $100.

### Osborne Apartments

Opened in 1885 for a wealthy clientele, the Osborne Apartments on West 57th Street had a croquet lawn on the roof.

### *New Yorker* Motto

The original motto of the *New Yorker* was: "Not for the Old Lady in Dubuque."

## Bible Study

A person can study the Bible in 2,167 different languages and dialects at the library of the American Bible Society, founded in New York in 1816.

When you see yourself as a New Yorker you talk faster, you walk faster, and you think faster. We want the rest of America to respect us and, if possible, even to love us.

— Ed Koch, former Mayor of New York

## Beethoven or Bust

A bust of Beethoven faces the band shell in Central Park.

## Puck Building

The Puck Building at the corner of Lafayette and East Houston streets, finished in 1899, has a sculpture of the Shakespearean character over the doorway.

## Cherry Tree

The world's largest Japanese cherry tree is located in the New York Botanical Garden in the Bronx.

# Love in the Balance

Two male lovers—a man in a black dress and a boy in a pair of shorts and no shirt—protested their families' lack of understanding for what they felt for each other by climbing a tree in Central Park and refusing to come down for hours. During those hours, a lot more than just hanging in the tree went on. The man, 32, played near the top of the tree, a 55-foot larch, while the boy, 17, sat quietly a few feet below. As crowds of onlookers appeared, the man stripped down to a thong and performed a sex act on the boy. One of the onlookers flagged down an officer on bicycle, and then the Emergency Services Unit officers appeared. The two men began to shout obscenities and throw branches down at the officers. Because the tree's largest branches were only four inches thick, the two men were at risk of falling so an inflatable safety mat was set up on the ground. Police negotiators went up the tree to talk the couple down. After about five hours, the police put harnesses on the lovers and began to pulley them down without protest. No one was injured and criminal charges are pending after their psychiatric evaluations.

## Homing Pigeons

Maspeth in Queens was long the center for the training of homing pigeons.

*It is an art form to hate New York City properly. So far I have always been a featherweight debunker of New York; it takes too much energy and endurance to record the infinite number of ways the city offends me.*

– Pat Conroy, *The Prince of Tides*, 1986

## A Dog's Life

At the latest count there were about 1 million dogs in the five boroughs. There are packs of roving wild dogs which, of course, have not been counted.

## Desperate for Fame

A mentally ill prison inmate threatened to kill the U.S. Senator for New York Hillary Clinton and was sentenced to an additional 18 months in prison—which is what he wanted. The man had written a letter to a prison psychologist in which he threatened to shoot a famous person. He gave a list of possible targets, including President Bill Clinton, his wife, and federal judges. The letter contained a detailed plan to shoot Hillary Clinton. The 52-year-old man who was serving a 30-month sentence for an unarmed bank robbery in New York, felt he had nothing to look forward to in the outside world and wanted his 15 minutes of fame—his criminal history stretched over 40 years and none of it was particularly newsworthy.

*Traffic signals in New York are just rough guidelines.*

– David Letterman

## Red, Amber, Green

There are 12,700 traffic lights in New York City. A traffic signal light bulb, on average, burns for 333 days.

## Traffic News

The average daily traffic volume in New York City is 2.3 million.

*New York is a catastrophe—but a magnificent catastrophe.*

– Le Corbusier, French architect

## City Cabs

There are 12,053 yellow cabs in the city. These are medallioned cabs and are regulated, whereas the roaming "gypsy" cabs are not. New York City cabs are required to take you where you want to go, but are not required to have change for anything larger than a $20 bill.

## Vehicles on the Move

At least 10,000 vehicles per day move onto First Avenue, headed for the F.D.R. or East River entrance ramp.

## The High Cost of Food on the Go

Concession stands are big business in New York. The annual rent for the hot dog and soda concession stand on the north side of the Metropolitan Museum of Art is over $300,000; for the south side, add another $25,000. While taxes are the city's number one source of revenue, these museum spots are ranked second. Other concession stand rents include close to $60,000 for Fifth Avenue and 72nd Street; Washington Square Park, with 6 carts at a total of close to $100,000; and Fifth Avenue and 60th Street, at the entrance to Central Park close to $100,000. The price for pretzels, soda, and hot dogs has gone up as well, but nowhere as much as at New York City's ballparks where a slice of pizza or a frankfurter can go for $4.75 each. And a grocery shopper in Manhattan pays 20 percent more for groceries than in any of the other boroughs.

## Carriage Birth

An average of 80 women go into labor on New York City subways each year.

## Get On Your Feet

An average of over 340,000 people walk to work each day.

## Tavern Opening

On the site of a sheepfold at 67th Street and Central Park West on October 20, 1934, Tavern on the Green opened—and it has been a mecca for tourists and natives alike. It featured stained glass windows, including one by Tiffany, and views of the Central Park gardens. It was closed briefly for renovation in 1972, then reopened, more extravagant than ever, with 45 new chandeliers, 14 new mirrors, and two new rooms: the Crystal Room and the Terrace Room.

Tavern on the Green serves an average of 2,000 people a day and employs 52 cooks. It takes a crew of seven full-time workers during the winter to put 400,000 tiny lights on the trees outside it.

Tavern on the Green marks the finish line of the New York City Marathon.

## Dragon Boat Festival

A person can rent a rowboat at Loeb's Boathouse in Central Park or participate in the Hong Kong Dragon Boat Festival. Entering its 15th year, this is the largest festival of its kind in the United States, with over 100 teams and over 1,000 participants from across the United States and Canada. Held at Meadows Lake in Queens, the dragon boat teams feature two days of racing as well as land events such as youth races, women's races, and Shaolin Temple warrior monks demonstrating kung fu. Dragon boat racing—where the boats are festooned with dragons similar to when the Chinese bring in their New Year—is one of the fastest growing competitive team sports in the United States. In New York, admission is free.

## North Moore Street

North Moore Street in TriBeCa was named for Benjamin Moore, the Episcopal bishop of New York in the early 1800s and the president of what was then Columbia College, now Columbia University. Bishop Moore was the father of Clement Clarke Moore, who wrote *The Night Before Christmas*.

I like the rough impersonality of New York, where human relations are oiled by jokes, complaints, and confessions—all made with the assumption of never seeing the other person again. I like New York because there are enough competing units to make it still seem a very mobile society. I like New York because it engenders high expectations simply by its pace.

– Bill Bradley, former U.S. Senator

## Empire State Lights

In 1964, the practice of floodlighting the upper stories of the Empire State Building began. The white lighting that is in place most of the year is turned off on foggy nights during the spring and fall to prevent birds from crashing into the building during migration season. The exterior lights stay on until 1 A.M.

Twenty different events or holidays prompt lightbulb color changes on the Empire State Building each year. These include a red, white, and blue combination for Independence Day, Lincoln's Birthday, Washington's Birthday, Memorial Day, Labor Day, and Veteran's Day. The lights turn purple for the Gay Pride Parade. A total of 255,000 watts illuminate 1,326 lights that bathe the spire in color from the 72nd to the 102nd floor.

## Campaign Fund Contributions

The zip code of 10021 on the upper East Side of Manhattan accounts for more federal and local campaign contributions than any other zip code in the United States. An average of $7 million is contributed by residents for campaign funds in federal elections.

## Toy Design

The Fashion Institute of Technology at Seventh Avenue and 27th Street opened in 1944 and is the only school in the world with a toy design department.

## Dancing in the Street

There are between 4,000 and 5,000 street fairs, block fairs, festivals, and parades each year in New York City.

## Rent-a-Toilet

It costs $75 a day to rent a portable toilet in New York City.

## Fish Market on Fulton Street

The Fulton Street Fish Market is the largest market for fish in the nation. The total weight of fish nightly is more than a million pounds and the market's annual revenue exceeds $1 billion.

## Car Architecture

On the Chrysler Building, there are gargoyles that depict Chrysler car ornaments and the spire is modeled on a radiator grille.

## Missouri Rockettes

The world famous Rockettes, long associated with Radio City Music Hall, were actually formed in St. Louis, and were originally named the Missouri Rockets.

# New York Animal

- New York City has the highest concentration of peregrine falcons in the world.

- The price per hour for an animal psychiatrist to attend to one of the Central Park Zoo's polar bears is $50.

- Pet massage therapy in New York City costs $60 an hour. The price for a portrait of one's pet can be as high as $15,000.

- The ferret was first brought to the United States in 1890 and was banned as a pet in New York City in 1990. The New York City Friends of Ferrets have been trying unsuccessfully to overturn the prohibition. The curator for the Bronx Zoo receives the most daily calls from owners wishing to get rid of their ferret.

- At the Bronx Zoo, 25 percent of the animals are on display at night. At Christmas, 300,000 lights are strung along the zoo's trees, in exhibition halls, and around animal sculptures for nighttime visitors.

## Pleasure Garden

Broadway and Ann Street was the location of the first "pleasure" garden in New York, called The Spring Garden. Pleasure gardens were an idea imported from England and were actually outdoor restaurants in a landscaped setting. The Spring Garden was begun in the early 1700s and lasted until 1768. Although there are many restaurants in New York City with outdoor tables for dining, the view is primarily sidewalk and skyscrapers. The Boathouse in Central Park is an exception as it overlooks the boating pond and the park.

*All of everything is concentrated here, population, theater, art, writing, publishing, importing, business, murder, mugging, luxury, poverty. It's all of everything. It goes all night. It is tireless and its air is charged with energy.*

— John Steinbeck, American writer

## Blimp Invasion

Five sunbathers at 410 West 53rd Street were enjoying themselves on tar beach: the roof of their apartment house. It was July 4, 1993, and their lazy afternoon was suddenly interrupted by a 160-foot blimp. The Bigfoot, as it was called, crash-landed on the roof then slowly circled downward as it lost helium. The $4 million blimp was on its maiden voyage across the country to advertise Pizza Hut's new 21-slice pizza. The pilot and co-pilot of the blimp were treated for minor injuries at a nearby hospital. None of the rooftop sun worshippers were hurt.

## Prohibition Park

In the Westerleigh area of Staten Island is a place called Prohibition Park. The first liquor distilled in the United States was brewed on Staten Island in 1640. In 1887, the National Prohibition Party bought a wooded 25-acre tract of land in what is now Westerleigh and called it Prohibition Park. It became a haven for teetotalers and the local temperance movement.

## Whispering Gallery

Many people have heard of the famous "whispering gallery" outside of the Oyster Bar in Grand Central Terminal. It is here that people standing at opposite ends of the hallway can hear each other's whispers. This occurs because the walls are shaped and curved in such a way that the sound follows the

*Many people have heard of the "whispering gallery" outside the Oyster Bar in Grand Central Terminal.*

contour of the wall around a gallery, bouncing across the surface, and reaching the listener's ears at almost the same volume. The spot by the Oyster Bar is where three passages meet beneath a vaulted ceiling, which is the ideal configuration for such a whispering gallery. There is also a small one at the base of the main staircase in Butler Library at Columbia University.

## Bronx Cheer

There is nothing so unpleasant as the sound of a Bronx cheer. Its genesis is the early part of the 20th century in a vaudeville theater in the Hub section of the Bronx. There was a vaudeville act so horrific that the audience booed it off the stage with a sound that was similar to "pfffft." A critic described the audience's reaction in a subsequent review as: "The act was so bad, they gave it the Bronx cheer." And forever after, it is the sound of utter and complete audience disapproval.

## Give 'Em a Hook

Unpopular stage performers not only heard how awful they were from the audience, they also saw it, thanks to the practice of giving a performer "the hook." The hook first appeared at Miner's Bowery Theatre, where in the 1890s amateur night was held every other Friday. Vaudeville was born on the Bowery stage, but they added a popular twist by offering a dollar to anyone willing to take the stage and perform, regardless of talent or ability. A precursor to karaoke, it would seem. Audience reaction soon became part of the entertainment. The less talented who took the stage were subject to an earsplitting cacophony of jeers and catcalls and heckling. To get the truly terrible acts off the stage as fast as possible, an inspired stage manager lashed a stage-prop shepherd's crook to a pole and started yanking the performers off the stage in mid-performance. The audience loved it, and "Give 'em a hook" became a favorite taunt.

> The less talented who took the stage were subject to an earsplitting cacophony of jeers and catcalls and heckling.

The Apollo Theatre was built at 125th Street in 1913, and in 1935, amateur night began there, showcasing some of the best and worst in entertainment. Among the best were Ella Fitzgerald and Sarah Vaughan. The worst got the hook. Amateur night is still held every Wednesday at the Apollo, without a hook.

## Down a Manhole

Manhole covers in New York City are made in India and China. They cost between $50 and $75 each and are round because square manhole covers could be lifted up, turned on their sides, and dropped down the shaft. That cannot be done with round ones.

## Turtle Power

A turtle the size of a manhole cover has been spotted coming out of Newtown Creek. Newtown Creek has the dubious honor of being the most polluted waterway in America. It is a murky estuary that runs 3½ miles along the border of Greenpoint, Brooklyn and Maspeth, Queens. Once a site for stately mansions, then a mecca for shipbuilding, it is now a toxic dumping ground that overflows with raw sewage every time it rains. Newtown Creek, as well as the ponds and marshes of all the boroughs, teem with giant snapping turtles which flourish, largely unseen, underwater, even if it's polluted water. They have been sighted in the salty tidal marshes of Jamaica Bay, the freshwater lakes of Central and Prospect Parks, and in the Hudson, East, and Bronx Rivers. Feeding on dead fish, small animals, and aquatic vegetation, the turtles, often covered with algae, can grow to weigh 35 to 40 pounds and measure 20 inches down the length of its dark brown shell. Snapping turtles, which have the power to crush with their jaws but are not aggressive, can live for 50 or 60 years.

## The Only Lighthouse in Manhattan

There is a classic children's book from 1942 called *The Little Red Lighthouse and the Great Gray Bridge* by Hildegard Hoyt Swift. This little red lighthouse is still in existence and is the only lighthouse in Manhattan. From 1880 to 1917, it was the North Beacon at Sandy Hook, New Jersey. Now it is on Jeffrey's Hook, a tiny outcropping from Fort Washington Park near 181st Street that extends into the Hudson River, at the foot of the George Washington Bridge. It was moved there in 1921 and still resides.

*New York makes one think of the collapse of civilization, about Sodom and Gomorrah, the end of the world. The end wouldn't come as a surprise here. Many people already bank on it.*

— Saul Bellow, *Mr. Sammler's Planet*, 1970

## Original Empire State Building

There are two Empire State Buildings, and the tall one that tourists flock to is not the original. The original was a nine-story structure at 640 Broadway and Bleecker Street built in 1897. Its name came from the tenant of the previous building at the site, the Empire State Bank. When the 102 Empire State Building opened, the other one began to be known by its address alone. Today, the building's original name inscription is covered by a piece of metal that says "640" and is home to a hot-dog shop and residential lofts.

## India House

On Hanover Square in the Financial District is a building with the words "India House" carved into its side. India House dates back to 1851 when it was built as a bank and then housed the New York Cotton Exchange. It was destroyed in the Great Fire of 1835. Today India House is an extremely private, almost secret club that has been in existence for over 85 years, and called India House because many of its first members traded goods with the Far East. All one really knows about the club is that it serves lunch.

## 33 Thomas Street

There is a tall, windowless building downtown that is incongruous with the architecture around it. The building at 33 Thomas Street is part of AT&T's huge Worldwide Intelligent Network, which directs an average of 175 million telephone calls a day. The building, 30 stories high, is filled with computers, and lacks windows to protect the machines, by cutting out the potential harm from the sun and making it easier to maintain a stable temperature within. The building's lack of windows also make it less vulnerable to other threats that have nothing to do with nature.

## Animal Oddities

In Herald Square where Macy's is located, there is also a memorial tower with a clock and some bronze birds. The location, on Broadway between 34th and 35th streets, was once attached to the building that housed the newspaper, the *New York Herald.* That building was erected in 1895 and demolished in 1921. In the 1940s, a base for the clock and birds was designed as a memorial to James Gordon Bennett, the newspaper's founder. The memorial depicts Minerva, the goddess of wisdom and invention, and at her side two bellringers, which is why the monument is sometimes referred to as the Bellringers Monument. The birds are two owls that contain bulbs and are set to timers for them to light up.

## Wild Boar

There is an odd statue of a wild boar in Sutton Place Park, which New Yorkers call a vest-pocket park located in one of Manhattan's most private, exclusive, and expensive neighborhoods. It is a replica of the bronze Wild Boar which was done by the Renaissance sculptor Pietro Tacca in 1634 and which can be found in Florence, Italy. Pigs, it seems, have long been considered interesting garden statuary, even in New York.

New York is the great stone desert.

– Israel Zangwill, British novelist

## Still Hunt

There is a carving of a giant cat crouched above the East Drive at 76th Street in Central Park, often scaring runners right out of their Nikes since it is partially hidden by trees and there's no pedestal to announce its presence as art. The bronze is called Still Hunt and was installed in 1881. The sculptor was Edward Kemeys who worked with the Parks Department's Corps of Engineers in the 1860s. He traveled around the United States looking for native beasts to sculpt. Still Hunt is an American mountain lion. His two African lions guard the gates of the Art Institute of Chicago.

## Gracie Mansion

Gracie Mansion was built in 1799 as the country estate of Archibald Gracie, a merchant from downtown because the Upper East Side at that time was considered the country. He used his 16-room house to entertain, but when his shipping business failed during the War of 1812, he was forced to sell. New York City bought the house in 1887 and used it as the Museum of the City of New York until 1942 when it became the official mayor's residence. Fiorello H. La Guardia was the new mayor, and his choice of residence was either Gracie Mansion or a 75-room French-style chateau on Riverside Drive. Ever since, Gracie Mansion has been home to New York City's mayors.

## Matinee Shows

Theater producers are allowed to put on eight shows a week before having to pay enormous amounts in overtime to union employees, so they spread out performances to maximize profits. Theaters are closed on Monday, have a Saturday matinee for the big crowds, and offer another matinee on Wednesday. At one point, major Broadway stars such as Lillian Gish, Shirley Booth, the Lunts, Helen Hayes, and Ethel Barrymore, preferred Thursday for their matinee performance. They were part of the influential Theater Guild, and when their power waned in the 1950s, Wednesday matinees became permanent.

### Begging Nuns

New York City has a few religious communities that practice panhandling as a means of fulfilling the vows of poverty. Some of these groups are nuns. Others are women who dress up in a habit and pose as nuns to collect the money. There is a way, however, to check the authenticity of a begging nun. Only the Archdiocese of New York's Vicariate for Religious Issues can approve begging. The office issues an annual mendicant card with an official seal, and only about five sisters apply for it annually. A nun must carry this card at all times to beg.

## Brooks Brothers

Brooks Brothers was established in New York in 1818. They introduced the first English-style silk neckties to the United States. In England, however, the stripes on a regimental tie go from top right to left whereas on a Brooks Brothers tie, the stripe goes from top left to right. This was a deliberate change to spare American customers from accusations that they wore English club ties to which they were not entitled. Today, Brooks Brothers carries 30 basic stripe-and-color combinations, each based on five old Brooks patterns, with names like No. 1, No. 2, and No. 3.

## Abercrombie and Fitch

Abercrombie and Fitch were retailers formed during the late 19th century as an outdoor-supply store by David T. Abercrombie, a railroad engineer. One of the first customers to the store on South Street in Manhattan was Ezra H. Fitch, a wealthy lawyer and sportsman who became Abercrombie's partner. In 1908, the store provided President Theodore Roosevelt with equipment for an African safari, including snake-proof sleeping bags. Abercrombie left in 1912 and Fitch moved the store to Madison Avenue at 45th Street in 1917, but kept the two names. A fly-casting pond was installed on the roof of the store and a shooting range was put in the basement, which was closed when a customer hurt his shoulder while firing an elephant gun. Occasionally Katharine Hepburn would ride a bicycle across the main floor.

## U Thant Island

In the middle of the East River, near the United Nations, is a tiny land mass called U Thant Island. It is less than half an acre in size, originally called Man-o'-War Reef. At the beginning of the 20th century, it was heaped with rocks and soil removed from a trolley tunnel begun under the river. In 1906, the tunnel was completed by August Belmont and used for the subway system. The island became known as Belmont Island, and is now owned by the city. Then, in 1977, a group of United Nations employees who were followers of Sri Chinmoy, a mystic from Queens, rechristened the island in honor of the Burmese diplomat U Thant, who was the third secretary general of the United Nations from 1961 to 1971. The Coast Guard keeps a 57-foot tower with a blinking green navigation light at the southern end, but except for followers of Sri Chinmoy who are allowed on the island a few times a year for maintenance, there are no visits to U Thant Island.

## Lost in the Park

Every lamppost in Central Park has a little metal plate attached to its base with a four digit number. The first two digits are the closest cross street and this serves two purposes: if someone gets lost in the park, they can determine the closest cross street, and the markers let maintenance workers identify which lights need repair.

## Arthur Kill

There is a tidal straight about 10 miles long between Staten Island and New Jersey known as Arthur Kill. Two islands in the waterway belong to Staten Island. One is Pralls Island, which is a bird sanctuary of 30 acres, and the other is the exact opposite of a sanctuary. It is called the Island of Meadows and sits at the entrance to Fresh Kills, the former garbage dump for the city.

## Greek Queens

Astoria, Queens, has the largest Greek population outside of Greece, and St. Demetrious, one of eleven Greek Orthodox churches in the area, is the largest outside of Greece.

## Weatherstar

In 1950, the Mutual of New York Insurance Company built their own skyscraper at Broadway and 56th Street. At the top of the MONY building is a blinking pole called the Weatherstar. It predicts the weather and is updated every six hours. If the lights are traveling upward, it signifies a warming trend; if down, then cooler.

## New York Slang

No one can make fun of another like a New Yorker. Creating slang words and phrases has been a New York pastime from the early 19th century, but this should not be too surprising. In the United States, different regions have different uses for the American language. There are parts of the South that have words and expressions—and are spoken in a twang—that is totally incomprehensible to the rest of America.

The wealthy were known in the 1840s as the Upper Ten (Thousand)—there were only enough of them at the time to be counted. Many of these same wealthy lived on Fifth Avenue—and still do. Fifth Avenue above 59th Street has some of the most exquisite and immense apartments and mansions in the world, with double digit price tags for purchase not unusual. By 1850, the rich on Fifth Avenue were known as Avenoodles, which was slightly derisive of the local pronunciation of "avenue" as two syllables instead of the correct three. In the 1880s, Astorbilt became a generic surname for the wealthy, the word being a combination of those two tycoons, Astor and Vanderbilt.

> *The rich have always been a rich source for New York slang. The words ritz and ritzy were inspired by the high style of the Ritz hotels.*

The rich have always been a rich source for New York slang. The words ritz and ritzy, and the phrase "puttin' on the ritz" were inspired by the high style of the Ritz hotels. To this day, on West 57th Street, there is the Ritz Thrift Shop which is anything but since it specializes only in fur coats and jackets, and is the place where society matrons bring their slightly used furs for resale.

During the 1890s, the wealthy were often called the Four Hundred. This phrase was coined by a society gentleman named Ward McAllister who, at one of Mrs. William Astor's parties, remarked that she had limited her guest list to four hundred. There is still a segment of New York society that can trace their lineage back to this time.

The regular folk also could give rise to new words and phrases. Chorus girls were often called Dumb Doras. And it wouldn't be surprising to see them accompanied by a sugar daddy who took them to after-show, late-night dinners of champagne and lobster at one of those lobster palaces that were so popular in Times Square.

New Yorkers borrowed from Britain and the Cockney verb to hook, meaning to solicit or prostitute. Hooker became a noun in New York in the 1840s with the proliferation of brothels in Corlear's Hook, where residents were known as hookers. At about this time, such expressions and words as ok, shyster, and smart aleck came into use. Then there was the expression developed in the 1860s and still being used to this day, of being "sent up the river." This meant going to Sing Sing Prison, which was a prison upstate on the Hudson River. One phrase that has disappeared from New York vernacular is "go peddle your papers" which used to mean get lost to the pesky newsboys hawking the daily papers.

The hokey-pokey man was the ice-cream vendor and then became the name of a popular song and dance for children. Most people have heard about yellow journalism which came about when Randolph Hearst and Joseph Pulitzer tried to outdo each other with extravagant headlines and muckraking stories. There are those who read the *New York Post* and *New York Daily News* today who believe nothing has changed since the 1880s.

Skyscraper was coined in New York, as was "to do a Brodie." This was in reference to the false claim of a saloonkeeper from the Bowery named Steve Brodie who claimed that he had dived, or tried to commit suicide, from the Brooklyn Bridge in 1886. Although the official name is frankfurter, hot dog has been around since the 1890s, because of the rumor started when they were first introduced that they were made with dog meat.

> Most people have heard about yellow journalism which came about when Hearst and Pulitzer tried to outdo each other with extravagant headlines.

Gawking tourists became known as rubberneckers. At the end of the 19th century and the beginning of the 20th, the elevated lines, or els, were so crowded at certain hours that those times became known as rush hour. And these commuters would stand on the trolley, holding on to overhead straps, inspiring the word straphanger. And it was in the beginning of the 20th century, not during the Depression later, that the term breadline was coined. Fleischmann's bakery had a shop on Broadway at 10th Street, and began giving bread and coffee away to the poor each night at its side door.

One of the most popular names to call someone in the 1940s was Herkimer Jerkimer, a snide reference to being a country bumpkin in the big city. Jerk became part of the lingo then and Herkimer referred to an upstate town in New York.

After World War I, nightlife was focused on those in Café Society, a name coined in a gossip column and in use through the 1930s. Younger members of society who had apartments were called cliff dwellers and the older folk, who lived in mansions, were known as cave dwellers.

A Broadway musical of the 1920s made popular the expression "makin' whoopee" to describe naughty behavior. The term G-string came about in the 1930s in burlesque, and was really the name of the loincloth used by a Native American man. Tarpaper beach refers to the tarred and graveled rooftops of apartment buildings where tenants sunbathe when they can't afford to go the beach. Dumbbell tenements was the name for apartments whose floor plan resembled a dumbbell. In the 1960s, homeless women became bag ladies. Yuppies was coined in the 1980s to describe people in their late 20s and early 30s, from the middle or upper class, who were into material things only. And with the advent of hip-hop, whole new dictionaries have been formed, adding to the lexicon such expressions as bad to mean good, and bling bling, which refers to the sound made by the heavy gold jewelry that hip-hop stars wear.

## Birdland

In December 1949, in a basement at Broadway and 52nd Street, the jazz club Birdland opened in tribute to the alto saxophonist Charlie "Bird" Parker. The club seated four hundred and was the site of performances by the biggest names in jazz, including Parker, Dizzy Gillespie, and Count Basie, among others. The club and its name became synonymous with New York City jazz until it closed in 1965 because of exorbitant rent hikes.

### Home of Punk Rock

In 1973, a rock club opened at 315 Bowery near Bleecker Street called CBGB (&OMFUG), which stood for: Country, Bluegrass, Blues, and Other Music for Uplifting Gourmandizers. As a country venue in the hip downtown scene of Manhattan, it failed. It reinvented itself in 1974 as a rock club and began to make music history, featuring performances by performers like the Ramones, B-52s, and Blondie. By the mid-1990s, CBGB was the best-known rock club in the country.

*New York City is a place halfway between America and the world.*

— George Bernard Shaw, British playwright and author

## Coogan's Bluff

*Coogan's Bluff* was the name of a film starring Clint Eastwood. It is also a neighborhood in northern Manhattan, known for its steep escarpment that descends 175 feet to sea level. The area was named for James Jay Coogan, a real estate merchant of the late 19th century, who twice ran unsuccessfully for mayor of New York. Among his property holdings was the Polo Grounds which was built in 1890 as Brotherhood Park. The stadium was home for a while to baseball's New York Giants and New York Mets.

## Diamonds are a Girl's Best Friend

The Diamond District is an area of midtown Manhattan on 47th Street between Fifth and Sixth avenues. It became the center of the retail and wholesale diamond trade in New York City when dealers and the Diamond Dealers Club, formed in 1931, moved north. The district grew in importance when Hitler invaded the Low Countries of Europe. Thousands of Jews fled the diamond centers of Antwerp, Belgium, and Amsterdam and settled in New York City. All transactions in the diamond district are closed with a handshake and the Yiddish words *mazel und brucha*, which means luck and blessing. Any disputes between dealers are settled by the Diamond Dealers Clubs which handles 80 percent of all the diamonds entering the United States.

## Odd Fellows

In 1819, a secret, ritualistic fraternal organization was formed in Brooklyn called the Independent Order of Odd Fellows (IOOF). By 1924, there were over 25,000 members in New York City in 157 lodges. The organization is a community-based charity that offers insurance for members and their families, supports heart research, is a summer camp for children with cancer, and funds the United Odd Fellow and Rebekah Home in the Bronx. Membership has decreased somewhat. Today there are not quite 12,000 members in the entire state of New York, with 27 lodges in Manhattan and 14 in Brooklyn.

The Lambs is another private club, this one formed in 1874 at Delmonico's restaurant by five men involved in theater. It is America's oldest professional theatrical club. The members met at various restaurants around Union Square before renting space on West 26th Street, and finally ending up for decades on West 44th Street in the theater district. Now it is located on West 51st Street right off Fifth Avenue. Members of the Lambs perform in monthly "Lambastes" as well as four annual stage shows which support their theater and the Lambs Foundation, which supports classes for actors. The club steward is called the Shepherd, the membership the Flock, and the clubhouse is the Fold.

# Gargoyles

New York City is a veritable treasure trove of gargoyles. Fish line the doorways of a building on Wall Street that also boasts a series of round medallions, featuring seahorses and mermaids. Gremlins and alligators line the doorway of another Wall Street building; maybe they bring luck and prosperity as the financiers fiddle with the funds. The famous Woolworth Building has a series of human heads and grotesque little imps decorate a building at Irving Place. Elsewhere in the city one can find winged gargoyles and cherubs, rams' heads, cornucopia baskets, lions, peacocks, and even hooded monk heads. All are part of the architecture, part of the weirdness.

## Pulling Strings

In 1919, the Manteo Sicilian Marionette Theatre opened in New York City. This was a form of puppetry developed in Sicily in the early 19th century. In 1894, the Manteo family of Sicily brought the show first to Argentina, and then to New York City. This was the only puppet show that used life-size marionettes and worked with the rod-control technique developed in early Roman times. The Manteo Sicilian Marionette Theatre was the first of its kind in America, housed first on the Lower East Side and then moving to Little Italy in 1923. The troupe performed Ariosto's *Orlando Furioso*, which was divided into 394 episodes requiring 13 months of nightly performances to complete. Admission was 25 cents. Miguel Manteo, the son of the founder, led the troupe until his death in 1990. Electricians by day, the family has performed for august institutions throughout America, including the Festival of American Folklife at the Smithsonian Institution. The troupe still exists and still performs, and is the last surviving company of its kind in North America.

## Moving Day

The English custom of celebrating May Day led to the practice in New York City of signing apartment rental leases on May 1, known for a long time as Moving Day. From the 19th century, New York has always suffered from a chronic housing shortage and high rents. This led tenants to move frequently, hoping to improve their situation. All trade ceased on May 1 because the streets were so heavily filled with traffic that no commerce could be conducted. After the 1873 financial depression, more housing was built and tenants began to move less often. Residential leases are now signed throughout the year. Commercial leases, however, are still effective on May 1 or, in keeping with the British tradition of paying land rents at Michaelmas, on October 1.

## The Legalization of Tattooing

After the City Health Department blamed tattooists for an outbreak of blood-borne hepatitis, tattooing was declared illegal in New York City in 1961. Nevertheless, it being New York, tattoos continued to be done, in condemned warehouses, basements, or backrooms of tenements. Rock and roll in the 1970s saw a resurgence of tattooing, and one well-known artist protested the ban by tattooing a porn star on the hallowed steps of the Metropolitan Museum of Art. He was arrested and charged with a medical misdemeanor. The tattoo artist appealed his case up to the New York Supreme Court who refused to hear it. In 1985, the New York Tattoo Society was formed in a Sixth Street gallery. It became a monthly meeting place for tattoo artists from across the city to share ideas and learn better techniques. Underground shops began to flourish as tattooing became popular throughout the country yet remained illegal in New York City—supposedly one of the more liberal cities in the country.

By 1995, some tattoo artists were taking out discreet ads in the back pages of alternative newspapers, and there were no repercussions from the law. They had to legitimize their business by dealing with the law, and it was the New York Tattoo Society that engineered the change that eventually came about in 1997. But first they had to fight. Kathryn Freed, a New York City council worker, learned that tattooing was illegal when one of her employees went to get one, so she decided to challenge the law. Clayton Patterson who heads the Society and

Wes Wood (a tattoo supplier and member) and the council worker struggled for almost a year by going to every tattoo shop in the city, speaking at City Hall, and holding meetings. City Council were about to have a vote on legalizing tattooing when the Society received a list of regulations they would require before legalizing. These regulations were largely restrictions, since they included a $5,000 licensing fee; restrictions on square footage of a tattoo parlor; even rules on the intensity of light bulbs and material for walls and floors. There was no question in Patterson's, Wood's, and Kathryn Freed's minds that they had to challenge what were obviously deliberate hindrances to the legalization of tattooing.

Support came from an unexpected source, the New York Health Department who determined that no regulations need be set upon the tattoo industry because there was no evidence any were needed: there had not been one single outbreak of blood-borne hepatitis since the ban in 1961. In 1997, by a vote of 38 to seven with one abstention, Local Law 12 requires only that tattoo artists be older than 18, with no convictions under state law for tattooing anyone under the age of 18. A tattoo artist in the city has to pass a Health Department examination and pay $100 every two years (not $5,000) for a license. Fines ranging from $300 to $1,000, depending on the offense, would be charged if a tattoo artist was found in violation of any of these rules. Tattooing is now a legitimate business in New York, so legitimate that in 2004, it held the first ever Tattoo Convention in the country.

# Cleopatra's Needle

Cleopatra's Needle is unique to New York City. It is a 69-foot red granite obelisk that resides in Central Park near the Metropolitan Museum of Art. Erected in Heliopolis in about 1475 B.C. by Pharaoh Thutmose III, Roman soldiers moved it in 12 B.C. to Alexandria where it remained until it was shipped to New York City in 1880 as a gift from the khedive, or Turkish viceroy, of Egypt. How it got from its arrival by Egyptian steamer in Staten Island to Central Park was a feat of ingenuity and muscle—and took four months. After arriving in Staten Island, it was towed on pontoons to the foot of 96th Street then placed on a cradle made of two joined beams attached to a pile-driver engine with a winch. Day and night, night and day, the engine pulled itself and its load forward by winding the chain around a drum that was in the engine to a block anchored in the street ahead. Work gangs cleared the way and periodically moved the block forward. Finally, 112 days after arrival, on January 5, 1881, the obelisk known as Cleopatra's Needle was placed where it has remained ever since. Another obelisk known as Cleopatra's Needle, a similar gift, is in London. No one has ever determined if there is the slightest connection to Cleopatra.

## The Baby Doctor

An incubator for premature babies used to be displayed with live babies at Coney Island. Dr. Martin A. Couney was educated in Paris by an early pioneer in the field of survival techniques for premature babies. Couney's teacher requested that his associate exhibit what he called an incubator at the World Exposition in Berlin, Germany in 1896. The exhibit was a huge success, drawing large crowds. In 1903, Dr. Couney emigrated to America, and was unable to persuade hospitals to adopt his techniques with premature newborns. Couney exhibited the incubator with live babies to prove his techniques every summer for the next 40 years on Coney Island. Nurses were employed to attend the babies and the public paid admission. Of 8,000 infants brought to Dr. Couney, 7,500 survived.

## PATH Route

Thousands of commuters use the PATH system daily, the Port Authority Trans Hudson. This is the supposedly cooperative management partnership between New York and New Jersey for what once was called "the haul and maul" or the Manhattan-Hudson Railroad.

## The Dakota

The famous Dakota apartment building at West 72nd Street is one of New York City's most coveted and well-known addresses. However, in 1884, when the sewing machine magnate Edward C. Clark decided to build here, the area was at the city's desolate northern fringe. Clark was derided for his choice of location, and it was labeled Clark's Folly, said to be so far uptown as to be in the Dakota Territory. Clark knew how to take an insult and turn it into an opportunity. He called his building The Dakota, and had such Dakota emblems as cornstalks and arrowheads carved in relief in the building.

## The God Box

On Riverside Drive between 119th and 120th streets stands the large, 19th-century Interchurch Center, also known as "the God box." It was dedicated in 1960 as a national symbol of Christian unity, providing offices for a variety of religious organizations and nonprofit agencies. Among the tenants are the United Methodist Church, the National Council of Churches, the Presbyterian Church, the American Baptist Churches, and the World Council of Churches. The building includes more than 500,000 feet of office space, a library, two art galleries, a chapel, and underground parking. About 1,800 people work in the squat cube of a building—hence its nickname—with row upon row of 1,289 identical four-by-six-foot windows. A third of the office space is rented by the ubiquitous Columbia University, and new tenants include Alcoholics Anonymous and the American Guild of Organists.

# SOURCES

Brett, Hy, *The Ultimate New York City Trivia*, Rutledge Hill Press, 1997.

Bunyan, Patrick, *All Around the Town: Amazing Manhattan Facts and Curiosities,* Fordham University Press, 1999.

Jackson, Kenneth T., *The Encyclopedia of New York City*, Yale University Press, 1995.

Kannapell, Andrea, and the editors of the *New York Times*'s "Fyi" column, *The Curious New Yorker: 329 Fascinating Questions and Surprising Answers about New York City,* Three Rivers Press, 1999.

Kim Taylor, B., *The Great New York City Trivia & Fact Book,* Cumberland House, 1998.